GIRL WARRIORS

GIRL WARRIORS

How 25 Young Activists Are Saving the Earth

RACHEL SARAH

CHICAGO
REVIEW
PRESS

Published by Chicago Review Press Incorporated
814 North Franklin Street
Chicago, Illinois 60610
ISBN 978-1-64160-371-3

Library of Congress Cataloging-in-Publication Data
Names: Sarah, Rachel, author.
Title: Girl warriors : how 25 young activists are saving the earth / Rachel
    Sarah.
Description: Chicago, IL : Chicago Review Press, 2021. | Includes
    bibliographical references. | Audience: Ages 9–12 | Audience: Grades 4–6
    | Summary: "Interviews with 25 climate leaders under age 25 present a
    hopeful picture of the future of environmentalism. These fearless girls
    and young women from all over the world have led hundreds of thousands
    of people in climate strikes, founded nonprofits, given TED talks, and
    sued their governments. They are standing up to demand change when no
    one else is"— Provided by publisher.
Identifiers: LCCN 2020049332 (print) | LCCN 2020049333 (ebook) | ISBN
    9781641603713 (trade paperback) | ISBN 9781641603720 (adobe pdf) | ISBN
    9781641603744 (epub) | ISBN 9781641603737 (kindle edition)
Subjects: LCSH: Women environmentalists—Biography—Juvenile literature. |
    Global warming—Juvenile literature. | Climatic changes—Juvenile
    literature. | Internet games—Juvenile literature.
Classification: LCC GE195.9 .S27 2021 (print) | LCC GE195.9 (ebook) | DDC
    333.72092/52—dc23
LC record available at https://lccn.loc.gov/2020049332
LC ebook record available at https://lccn.loc.gov/2020049333

Cover and interior design: Sadie Teper
Cover illustrations: Ana Copenicker

Printed in the United States of America

5 4 3 2 1

This book is for all of the Warriors in the world,
including my own,
Mae and Camille.

Thank you to the activists in this book for
sharing your hopes and your struggles,
giving your time,
trusting me.
You are the real storytellers.

xoxo,
Rachel Sarah

Contents

Introduction

As I write this, it is 9:00 on a summer morning in northern California. It should be bright and sunny, but the sky is filled with smoke from wildfires that are raging across the entire West Coast. I'm watching the culmination of centuries of human disregard for our environment. The ash is so thick it blocks out the sun, letting in only a dark orange-reddish hue. It might as well be evening.

We've been sheltered at home for months as COVID-19 spreads, and now the wildfires are burning again. My younger daughter has moved into my bed because she's so worried. In the dark, I get up to work on this book when my older daughter walks in, looks at the sky, and says, "How can everyone go on like this is normal?"

We can't. The girls and young women in these pages know this. They have grown up in crisis, watching as the adults around them destroy the Earth. From a young age, they've spoken up about the violence, racism, and greed they've witnessed. That's why I wrote this book: to amplify the voices of young climate activists from around the world.

Climate change is without a doubt the biggest crisis humanity has ever faced. By 2018, when Greta Thunberg began her School Strike for Climate at age 15 in Sweden, the media had begun to wake up. A little. But Greta hasn't been alone in this fight. Thousands of activists around the world—some inspired by Greta, others who've been fighting for the climate since before

Greta's time—have been speaking out, rising up, and demanding their leaders take action.

Their stories inspired me and, in an increasingly scary world, gave me hope. So in 2019, I wrote an article for the *Washington Post* about teen climate activists in the United States hustling to save the planet. Until this point, my reporting had not focused on the climate, but that article sparked the idea for this book. My goal was to spend six months interviewing 25 climate activists under age 25 from around the globe.

I thought the hard part of writing this book would be finding activists, but every time I interviewed someone, I heard, "Oh, you should speak to so-and-so!" They led me to one another. They also introduced me to their moms, dads, siblings, and close friends. I spoke to girls and young women from the United States, Pakistan, Iran, Colombia, the Dominican Republic, Brazil, Jamaica, the Marshall Islands, Indonesia, Kenya, Uganda, England, Ireland, the Netherlands, India, and Australia.

These activists are fighting for the world they have inherited. Their age does not deter them. During my interviews, they reminded me: there can be no climate justice without racial justice. I'm a White, middle-class woman, and part of writing this book has been unlearning my own internalized privilege. My older daughter is Black, but still, the lens through which I write is a White, privileged one.

One of the rules that my first editors—all White men—taught me in the newsroom was: never share your story with a source before publication. Yes, you can verify quotes by reading them out loud, but if you share your story with a source, you'll no longer be in control of it. But how are these rules upholding a system that has kept White people in a position of power throughout history?

With the support of Kara Rota, my editor at Chicago Review Press, I sent the stories to every activist before publication. I'm grateful for their corrections, and for the times they pointed out places where I needed to say more.

As I finished writing this book, I cast my vote for the 2020 US presidential election. Then, along with the rest of the world, I waited as our heroic poll workers counted the votes. (And then I waited some more!) When my older daughter yelled out "Joe Biden won!" I felt so much relief and joy. We did it!! I'm *so* ecstatic that Kamala Harris is our first-ever Black woman vice president!

We have much more work to do. Every activist knows this. Interviewing and writing about these 25 Girl Warriors has changed me. We can't go on like this is normal. We need to fight for this planet, for the future, and for the futures of all children. We need to rise up in our resilience. I hope that reading their stories will stir something deep inside you too, and inspire you to create a new future.

Daphne Frias

Born: January 13, 1998
Lives: West Harlem, New York, United States
Loves: Crafting
Instagram: @frias_daphne
Pronouns: she/her/hers

On September 20, 2019, Daphne Frias was scheduled to be one of the official spokespeople for New York City's climate strike. The strike was supposed to start in in the Battery, a park 10 miles from her apartment in Harlem, which is practically on the other side of Manhattan. Daphne wasn't sure how'd she'd make it there. She gets around in a wheelchair, and because fewer than half of all subways in New York City are wheelchair accessible, taking the train was not an option. There was no way a cab would make it through the already crowded streets in time, but she refused to give up. If there's one word to describe Daphne, it's determined. She called a cab to drop her off as close as possible to the march.

From there, support showed up in the form of a tall guy named Sammer, who helped clear a path through the quarter of a million people in the streets so Daphne could get to the front of the march. Amy Goodman from Democracy Now! would be waiting there to interview Daphne.

Along the route, Daphne laughed as she rolled past everyone. "There are so many people!" she gushed. "It's so beautiful!" Instead of stressing out about how she'd reach the stage on time, Daphne was euphoric. She squeezed through the crowd and cheered. She smiled at strangers and waved to babies in strollers. Daphne absorbed the energy all around her. She basked in the chaos.

"People with disabilities are really affected by climate change," Daphne said that day during one of her news interviews. "We don't have the privilege to be able to up and leave when a natural disaster occurs."

Daphne was born in West Harlem, and doctors told her mom that her baby might not survive. That's because Daphne came into the world when she was only 27 weeks old, weighing just over a pound. That's the same weight as only two oranges!

"I was a tiny little thing, so I was in the hospital for three months," Daphne says. "My mom tells me stories about doctors needing to use their face masks for my diapers. I only had a 25 percent chance of survival, they said."

When Daphne was three years old, she was diagnosed with cerebral palsy (CP), the most common physical disability in childhood, which affects kids' movement, muscle tone, or posture. Every hour, a baby is born with CP, and there's currently no known cure.

When Daphne was a baby, doctors were not sure if she'd ever walk, but she sure could talk! Ever since she said her first words, Daphne has been asking questions and speaking up.

In her last year of preschool, Daphne was determined to walk. Without telling her mom, Daphne's teachers practiced with her every day, preparing for her graduation. The day came, and "I was so excited," Daphne says. "I stood up and walked. I did it!

"My mom started bawling," she adds.

"Daphne has always been very determined," her mom, Josie, says.

Daphne's parents are from the Dominican Republic, so she and her sister and brother grew up speaking Spanish at home. Daphne learned English in public school in New York City, where she went until third grade. That year, Daphne had an accident that fractured her knee. "I was in a cast for six weeks, and after they took the cast off, I lost my range of motion. We were all so confused, because I'd been walking before this, and now I couldn't walk at all."

Daphne went from one doctor to another for a year, traveling around by bus, train, and subway to find answers. "They said I should never have been put in a cast." Daphne had lost her muscle strength. Over the next two years, she went to rehab and had her first surgery, but the mobility in her legs didn't come back.

"Although I was born disabled, I was still able to walk in my own way until that accident," Daphne says. "After multiple extended stays in rehab, I was able to walk again using a walker and crutches. This was just as I was entering high school, and for the first time, I was contemplating my future. Therapy required me to attend multiple times a week if I wanted to walk again."

Between therapy and rehab, Daphne attended an elite high school in New York City. "I had six to seven hours of schoolwork each night, which didn't leave much room for therapy. My education is so important to me. I've always known that I wanted to be a doctor. I had to take high school seriously in order to pave the way for medical school."

Daphne says she struggled to keep up with the rigorous commitments of going to both school and therapy. "For a long time, I believed I had to walk to be successful," she says, explaining that she worked hard to break "that unhealthy mindset that I used to be in."

"Being disabled has brought many challenges in my life; the greatest one was when I decided to redefine my journey as someone with a disability," Daphne says.

After graduating from high school, Daphne went to college to study biology and anthropology as a double major, with minors in sociology and creative writing. "I've always loved to learn," she says. "I just love knowing things and asking questions."

In college, Daphne also organized students from her campus to travel to the nearest March for Our Lives event to rally for gun violence prevention.

In 2018 she was appointed as the New York State director for March for Our Lives.

She describes herself as an "organizer, advocate, storyteller, and peace builder. I am an unapologetically fierce Latina, who is proudly disabled. I zoom around on four wheels, fighting for social justice."

Her mom is her biggest supporter. "Watching her all these years, calling every doctor and every insurance company, she showed me what it means to be an activist," Josie says.

Her dad is a military veteran, and he "isn't very supportive of my activism," Daphne says. "He's a hard-core Republican. He doesn't believe in climate change or gun control. The military made him very conservative. But it's made me a better activist because I've had to work harder to find the middle ground."

Daphne says her parents both raised her in the same way, which is "If you have a question, you ask it." That's exactly what Daphne did when she wrote to her local city council representative—in 63 different letters!—to ask him to pass a climate emergency resolution. "He finally called me after three months, and the resolution passed that summer. I really think we need to remember that our elected officials work for us. They're supposed to represent us."

Daphne also spoke up for the Latinx and lower-income families in her community who live near fossil fuel plants and garbage waste centers. "I feel extremely compelled to speak up for the injustices that my community is facing," she says. These injustices are at the root of environmental racism, a system in which people of color bear a much greater burden from unsafe and unhealthy living and working conditions, waste and pollution, and environmental hazards.

At age 21, Daphne decided to run for office to be a county committee representative for her community, District 70 in Harlem. Daphne's mom and aunt both pitched in to get signatures on a campaign petition and posted fliers. "Daphne did the rest on the corner, speaking to people," Josie says.

Daphne won the election. She now runs a staff of four people on a county committee for West Harlem, where she serves as an elected liaison between the community and elected officials. "My office is six blocks from where I live, and my staff are all women of color under age 25."

Daphne is often tethered to her phone, tweeting at all hours, because social media is such a big part of where change happens. "Sometimes I tell her she has to turn off her phone," her mom says. "You need to power off for one day." Daphne agrees, even if it's not easy for her to put her phone down. "It's really hard sometimes, and I know I need to take care of myself. Two years ago, I was diagnosed with anxiety and depression, and that made me step back a little."

Stepping back isn't always easy for Daphne. But when she does, you can find her crafting. Anything DIY has her name all over it. "I've always loved art and doing things with my hands, because it's the one place where I feel like I don't have to be perfect."

In March 2020, Daphne was diagnosed with COVID-19. Because she has cerebral palsy, Daphne knew she could be at risk if she were exposed. Doctors gave her special treatments to keep her lungs open and her fever down. She was determined to get healthy. When she felt strong, she got back to crafting in her living room. "My disability doesn't determine what I do in life. It doesn't stop me from being who I am."

In spring 2020, Daphne found out that she'd been jointly accepted to both a medical school and a school of public health in Maryland. "This will allow me to fulfill my dream of earning my doctor of medicine and masters of public health," Daphne says. "Public health is so important to me, and I believe that social justice is public health too, because social justice is a public health crisis."

Saoi O'Connor

Born: October 31, 2002
Lives: Skibbereen, County Cork, Ireland
Loves: Walking their dogs at the beach and climbing barefoot over the rocks by the ocean to feel the sea spray
Instagram: @saoioconnor
Pronouns: they/them/their

Saoi was baking homemade bread in their kitchen in West Cork, Ireland. After mixing the dough and leaving it to rise, Saoi worried. It should've been rising faster. If not, it would turn out too dense.

Since they were a child, Saoi has worried a lot. "I've been aware of world issues like climate change and food justice since I was very young," Saoi says. "My parents taught me."

Saoi describes themself as "a very curious, highly overempathetic child who grew up with the internet and a wealth of books at my disposal." More often than not, Saoi was reading a new book or looking up the answer to a question. Saoi's name means "wise person" in Irish.

In the meantime, if this dough didn't rise, Saoi would try again tomorrow. That's what Saoi does.

They live on more than 26 acres of organic land in southern Ireland.

Lush, green, rolling hills surround their home. "My family also has chickens!" Saoi says. "We named them after Lord of the Rings characters."

"In this part of the world, where you're surrounded by so much life, everyone cares deeply about the environment," says Saoi's mom, Isolda, who's a speech and language pathologist. Saoi's dad is an accountant who works from home, so the family usually pauses to eat lunch together.

It is a two-hour bus ride from Saoi's home in the green, rolling hills to downtown Cork, the city where they've been striking on the steps of city hall every Friday since January 2019. Saoi was one of the very first climate strikers in Ireland.

At the beginning, Saoi was alone with the sign they'd painted in black letters on a white placard. THE EMPEROR HAS NO CLOTHES, it says. "I'm sure you know the fairy tale by Hans Christian Andersen," Saoi says. "Two weavers go to the emperor and promise him a new suit of clothes." The weavers know how much the emperor loves to wear new outfits and how little he cares about the people he is supposed to represent. The weavers tell the emperor that the new clothes will be invisible to anyone who is ignorant or not fit for office.

"In reality, they make no clothes at all," Saoi explains. But when people see the emperor walking around naked, they say nothing because they are afraid of looking foolish—until a child cries out, "The emperor has no clothes!"

In other words, youth like Saoi are the ones around the world who dare to point out the inconvenient truths to grown-ups.

Saoi adds their own meaning to the classic story: "We all pretend like something is happening as we see policies being made and motions being drafted. We hear things over the radio, say, about the Paris Agreement or record-high temperatures, yet leaders are unwilling to change the way we're living on this planet."

During the winter, Saoi showed up to city hall wearing tights under their pants and three layers of socks. Their fingers went numb from the cold, but by the time the seasons changed and the weather warmed up, everyone who worked inside city hall recognized Saoi. "Oh, you're the one who's out here for seven hours every Friday," the workers started to say.

If it wasn't raining or too cold, a handful of friends sometimes joined Saoi to strike. If someone had baked, vegan cupcakes or brownies got passed around to share. "Now, people who work at city hall bring us water, and they've told us we could use their bathroom," Saoi says.

During those first few months of striking, Saoi connected with Greta Thunberg in Sweden. Greta sent a video of support to Saoi and other Cork climate protesters, saying to them, "You have our full support and we stand behind you and we are very grateful that you are fighting for everyone's future and don't give up—never stop. Thank you."

Together with other climate activists in Europe, Saoi helped organize several global climate strikes that took place in March 2019. In Ireland alone, more than 15,000 people came out to the streets for that protest.

Six months later, in the fall of 2019, Saoi found themself face to face with Ireland's climate minister, Richard Bruton, talking about the nation's strategy to fight the crisis. Ireland needs to do more to value the lives and futures of young people, Saoi explained.

Due to the COVID-19 global pandemic, Saoi's travel plans were put on hold, including planned trips to the United Nations to discuss climate change. "Both COP [the 26th United Nations Climate Change Conference] and SB 52 [the Bonn Climate Change Conference] have been postponed until 2021, so there were no negotiations in 2020, which is a huge blow for us, as this should have been a really critical year," Saoi says.

The coronavirus hasn't distracted Saoi from their 24-7 job as climate activist at home. Every day, Saoi networks, plans, and organizes via social media and Zoom. When asked to describe how they see their role in the climate movement, Saoi says, "As a rule, I believe it's not about me."

One afternoon, they wrote a post on Instagram addressed to a "younger, quieter me":

Dear girls, Do not ever make yourself small.

*People who have never believed in anything, who have never had to
fight for anything, will always be afraid of women who speak their
minds.*
They will call you a b---h—let them. Be angry.
Take up space. Deep breath, be brave.
Love, Saoi.

In March 2020, during the pandemic, the *New York Times* contacted
Saoi to ask about striking online during the global pandemic. "Intersecting
crises will be a feature of our times," Saoi said. "We can't let one action stop
the other."

Maya Penn

Born: February 10, 2000
Lives: Atlanta, Georgia, United States
Loves: Storyboarding
Instagram: @mayasideas
Pronouns: she/her/hers

"Bring it here, Maya," her mom said. "Let's have a look."

Eight-year-old Maya had been playing in the garden at her home in Atlanta, Georgia, when her jeans ripped at the knee. She ran back inside to show her mom, thinking it was the end of her favorite pants. But her mom, Deidre, turned on the sewing machine and quickly patched up the knee. "There you go! As good as new."

"As I watched her fix it, I wanted to learn," Maya says.

That was when Maya's mom began teaching her daughter to sew by hand. "From there, I started to find material around the house and turn it into something new," Maya says.

Maya was in second grade when she began designing headbands with material she found around the house; soon she moved on to accessories such as scarves, hats, bags, jewelry, and more. You name it, Maya made it. She sketched designs, cut out the fabric, and sewed away. People stopped her on the street to ask where she'd purchased her outfits. "That's when I told my mom that I wanted to start my own business. She never tried to talk me out of it or tell me why I couldn't," Maya says.

In 2008, when Maya was eight years old, her mom helped her found Maya's Ideas, "eco-friendly handmade clothing and accessories," from her home. Maya uses recycled, organic, and vintage materials. She colors her fabrics with herbal teas.

That spring, Maya's family also planted seeds to start an organic garden in their backyard. "My mom had grown up in North Carolina with a garden. She wanted me to have that experience too. I always felt so proud when going out to pick our own strawberries, carrots, and herbs. The birds would always steal our blueberries, so I was glad if I got some blueberries."

Maya was unstoppable. If she wasn't sewing, she was sketching. "Ever since I could hold a crayon, I loved to draw." She taught herself how to make flip-books and made up stories with her own characters. By the time her dad gave her his old MacBook, she was ready to dive in and design on the screen.

Maya was 10 when *Forbes* magazine contacted her for an interview about her eco-clothing company. "I basically started my own business out of curiosity, but now it's real," she told the reporter, adding that she also "dreamed of becoming a digital animator someday."

By this time, Maya's mom had started to homeschool her, and she soaked up everything she could. "My family has always lived eco-consciously, recycling, conserving electricity and water. So I had that awareness of the impact I had on the planet. Out of curiosity I started doing my own research about the impact of the fashion industry on our planet. I discovered the impacts of the fast-fashion industry, overconsumption of natural resources, and usage of toxic dyes. Did you know the fashion industry produces more carbon emissions than all international flights and maritime shipping combined?"

The more Maya learned, the more she wanted to give back to the Earth and her community. "Sustainability is something I wanted to make a priority no matter what I did in life. So I really took environmental activism and ran with it on my own, especially for those who are deeply affected by environmental issues, like Black, Brown, and Indigenous communities."

Maya decided to give 10 to 20 percent of her profits to local and global charities in the southern United States, as well as to environmental groups and women's and girls' rights organizations. She founded a nonprofit called Maya's Ideas 4 the Planet.

"I saw her compassion take action at a very early age," says Deidre, her mom. "When she saw local news stories of people in need and injustices, she always wanted to know what she could do to help."

For example, when Maya read about girls in other countries who couldn't go to school during their monthly periods because they didn't have pads or sanitary items—which sometimes led to them having to drop out—she decided to design and create reusable, washable sanitary pads. She partnered with two organizations based in Georgia, MedShare and Youth Action Without Borders, to send thousands of pads to Haiti, Senegal, Cameroon, and Somalia.

Maya's phone didn't stop ringing. When she was 16 years old, she was commissioned to produce and create an animated film for the first-ever digital report presented to Congress. The report was created to get a women's history museum built in Washington, DC.

That year, the talk show host and TV producer Oprah Winfrey also called Maya. Oprah had chosen Maya as the youngest of the SuperSoul 100 entrepreneurs—*entrepreneur* means someone who manages a business.

"I believe that all people have been blessed with their own power, their own place, and their own way to positively impact the world," Maya says. "Be creative, be curious, and watch as your awesomeness is unleashed."

These words sparked the title of Maya's book, *You Got This! Unleash Your Awesomeness, Find Your Path, and Change Your World*, published by Simon and Schuster in 2016. The book teaches young entrepreneurs about growing and giving back.

For every interview or talk Maya gives, she wears vintage or second-hand clothing. Maya says, "I usually alter whatever I have, to make it fit and to add something for fun. That's just the way I am!"

Maya has given three TED Talks so far about her life and her business.

She was 12 when the TEDWomen conference invited her to speak; she's the youngest female ever to do two back-to-back official TED Talks. Her talk about becoming an entrepreneur at age eight has been viewed online nearly 1.9 million times.

During one of her TED Talks, Maya premiered a clip of an animated show she has been working on, about the importance of bees and other pollinators. She describes *The Pollinators* as "a superhero team fighting the bad guys who harm the Earth. It teaches kids they can make a difference." After developing the concept further into an environmental adventure fantasy story, Maya is now producing it as a short film through her own production company.

Every week, Maya juggles designing, sewing, and animating her own series. Meditating is what grounds Maya. "I'm a visual person and have an active imagination, so meditation helps," she says. "It's how I start every morning, with visualization, mindfulness, and breathing. It's so important!"

Major fashion brands have hired Maya as a consultant as they shift into more eco-friendly practices to reduce waste.

"I really admire Maya for who she is as a person and how she lives by her truth," Maya's mom says.

"My mom has always been the ultimate cheerleader," Maya says. "Whether it's helping me pack before flying out to give a TED Talk or just keeping me grounded, she's my rock, and she's been my biggest supporter on my journey through all my years of activism as well as my journey growing up."

Today, when Maya speaks to audiences, she reminds them that it's time to face the racial injustices in the world. She urges people to understand the history of racial injustice in the United States so we can change the system in this country.

"Systemic racism is the foundation of what the United States is built upon," Maya says. "You see it in police brutality, environmental racism, the education system . . . It's so important for allies to move with knowledge, heart, and a persistence in doing what is right, because we have to shape a better, more equal world for future generations to thrive in."

Selina N. Leem

Born: November 12, 1997
Lives: Seattle, Washington, United States
Loves: Writing
Instagram: @_lipuppy12
Pronouns: she/her/hers

Fifteen-year-old Selina had an assignment due for school, but she didn't have any poster paper to do the project.

"My family is not well off," Selina says. "We didn't have the money, so I went to my school to see if they could help me."

Selina was born and raised in Majuro, the capital city of the Republic of the Marshall Islands, an island chain in the Pacific Ocean halfway between Hawaii and Australia. In the office of her high school in Majuro, Selina asked if someone might have some extra poster paper. The school administrator said no, there was no extra paper. So she asked if she might, at the very least, print out her poster so she could turn in something to her teacher. Again, the answer was no.

"I was mad at the school and the Ministry of Education," Selina says. "As one of the top two to receive the highest funding from the United States government through the Compact of Free Association agreement, I did not understand how our school was so lacking in supplies."

Selina headed to the library to print out her assignment, but the printer there was out of paper and ink. So she headed to her counselor's office. "But they told me they couldn't use my flash drive, because their computer might get a virus. It was really frustrating. Where were these millions of dollars going? Why was there no bloody ink and paper in the library? Why was no one fighting for our case?"

That week, Selina's teacher deducted 20 percent from her grade for not turning in her project on poster paper. "It was maddening," she says. "I thought, *You can't do this to me*. I needed good grades so I could go to a good university. Who else was going to provide for my family?"

In that moment, Selina saw everything that was wrong with the education system. So, that night, she wrote a letter to the Ministry of Education, explaining that the lack of funding made it impossible for her to complete her school assignments. Selina posted her letter on Facebook. "The next thing I knew, it ended up on the front page of the *Marshall Islands Journal*," she says, referring to her local newspaper.

Selina had raised her voice for all young people on her island, even if that's "very against our culture," she says. "In our society, young girls are not supposed to get into adults' business."

Her family worried that Selina had offended the elders on the island. "Girls are supposed to focus on their household chores and leave the leading to the boys," Selina explains. "But then, a couple of weeks later, my friends told me to go to the school office. An entire wall was covered with stacks of paper and ink." Thanks to her letter, the Ministry of Education had sent over a bunch of supplies to her school!

Tamara Greenstone Alefaio, an educator who'd relocated to the Marshall Islands from Vancouver, Canada, years earlier, had been following the news about Selina. So when Selina approached Tamara, asking if she could join her Model United Nations club, "she was already a little notorious," Tamara says. The two quickly formed a deep connection, and Tamara encouraged Selina to apply for a scholarship to study abroad.

Selina was 16 when the United World Colleges' Robert Bosch College offered her a spot in its international program in Freiburg, Germany. Selina was so excited, because she'd be able to finish high school with teens from around the world, and she'd be studying sustainability.

Selina had grown up experiencing the effects of climate change on the Marshall Islands, where the sea levels have been rising every year, causing the islands to slowly disappear. But it was the experience of moving away from home that gave Selina the time and space to really study and talk about the climate crisis. She was determined to tell people in wealthier nations, like Germany, about how the poorest island nations are bearing the brunt of emissions from the richer countries.

While she was in Germany, Selina was invited to speak at a climate strike. By the year 2030, Selina told the crowd, her country could be wiped out from rising sea levels. She described how warming temperatures made it impossible for coral reefs and fish to survive.

As a result of this speech, people started to hear about Selina and invite her to speak. Whereas Selina had become notorious in her community for speaking out, now she was being applauded for her advocacy. In her senior year of high school, she was even invited to be the youngest member of a delegation being formed to represent the Marshall Islands at COP21, the 2015 UN Climate Change Conference in Paris.

In his closing remarks, the late Tony deBrum, then minister of foreign affairs of the Republic of the Marshall Islands, passed the mic to Selina. "If this is a story about our islands, it is a story for the whole world," Selina told the leaders of 195 countries. "Sometimes when you want to make a change, then it is necessary to turn the world upside down. Because it is not for the better, but it is simply for the best." The audience gave Selina a standing ovation.

Selina's reputation as a powerful speaker increased. Invitations started to stream in from around the world. "People wanted to hear a Marshallese voice and their stories," Selina says. Meteorologist and author Eric Holthaus tweeted that Selina "is one of our world's most powerful voices on climate and gender and social justice."

After finishing school in Germany, 18-year-old Selina got an internship as an international educator at the United World College in Changshu, China.

In 2016 the Marshall Islands suffered a severe drought, and Selina's friends wrote to her in China, describing how they had to ration water every day. Selina worried about being so far away. She often turned to her journal to remember what she loved about home, like hearing the crickets at night. "I always thought growing up with my grandparents that our house was silent," she says. "But now I see that is not the case. Noise, nature's noise, is prevalent in its percussion silence, if that makes sense? Those were my lullabies growing up."

Selina's journal is always with her. "I write down what I'm grateful for during the day, like the sound of the waves billowing my curtains as I go to sleep, the smell of salt in the air, and even the pungent smell of seaweed."

In 2019 the Global Citizen Festival invited Selina (along with two other climate activists, Alexandria Villaseñor and Xiye Bastida) to New York City, where American actor and producer Leonardo DiCaprio introduced them to a crowd in Central Park. The crowd was so big that it equaled the population of the Marshall Islands!

"My island home in the Marshall Islands is already experiencing the effects of climate change and sea level rise," Selina said, speaking into the mic as her voice echoed over the ocean of people. "It could be uninhabitable by the time I'm 50 years old. Our leaders must do more! We demand that you do your part now."

Selina wants people to speak up and to push for political change. "The Republic of the Marshall Islands encompasses 34 islands and atolls. The Marshallese population would love to have all intact and safe."

Tamara, Selina's mentor with whom she has stayed in touch, says that Selina at her core is "tenacious, determined, loving, deep, honest, and sincere." Together, they've worked to get Selina into college, one of her biggest life dreams. In 2019, Selina was supposed to start college in New Zealand, but her scholarship fell through, and then her visa was declined. So she has settled in Seattle, where she's attending community college with the plan of transferring. "I still hope to do my bachelor's in New Zealand," she says. "I want to focus on Pacific studies, theater, and creative writing." Why Pacific studies? "Away from home, I realized how much I did not know about my region. I would always refer to Google for help. As I am becoming increasingly involved in climate warrior work, it is important that I am well equipped with knowledge of my region."

Selina is grateful to be in school, but she misses her community in the Marshall Islands. "Back home, more young people are becoming vocal and calling out our leaders to change," she says. "They are no longer waiting for the elders to speak on their behalf. They are taking things into their own hands. It makes me really happy. I cannot be any prouder of how far we have come."

Elsa Mengistu

Born: August 7, 2001
Lives: Washington, DC, United States
Loves: Traveling
Instagram: @elsamengistu
Pronouns: she/her/hers

When 18-year-old Elsa called her family in High Point, North Carolina, from her dorm room at Howard University in Washington, DC, she tried to keep calm. Her mom picked up the phone, and Elsa did not want to let on about the big surprise she had up her sleeve.

Elsa had just received an invitation to speak at a youth conference in Italy about sustainability. She was ecstatic to tell her mom, Alemitu, the news. But for now, she kept it under wraps. It was all good because Elsa's mom was already asking her a bunch of questions about her upcoming trip, the kind of questions any mom would ask when her daughter was about to travel abroad alone.

Fifteen years earlier, Elsa's parents had moved with three-year-old Elsa and her older brother and sister from Ethiopia to North Carolina, where they'd made a new home and had another baby. Alemitu had done everything she could to help her kids thrive and feel safe.

"I grew up in the South, where some people are very conservative," Elsa says. "You see Confederate flags everywhere and hear some ignorant views. This is what first got me advocating."

In sixth grade, Elsa fell in love with social studies. "It was the only thing I cared about that year. Then, by the time I got to seventh grade, we'd watch CNN on TV—well, the student version—and my teacher would let me debate for 20 minutes every day in front of the class. I guess that's how it all started"—*it* being Elsa's concern about justice. During middle school, Elsa debated everything in class, from gun control to racial injustice in the United States.

Elsa's younger sister, Etegenete (called Eta), says that when they were little, whenever Elsa "got a feeling that something was wrong, she'd stand up for that person."

Eta, who's four years younger than Elsa, followed her sister to the same high school. Eta says that whenever teachers saw her last name, "they'd ask if I was Elsa's sister, and they'd all rave about her. She was that kid who knew all of the teachers."

Alemitu says that since Elsa was a little girl, she was always asking questions. "Smart" and "confident" are two words her mom uses to describe her. "When we moved here from Ethiopia, she would always help people."

Her parents encouraged Elsa to go to medical school and become a doctor, "but Elsa told us that her mission is to be 'a human protector,'" her mom says.

When Elsa started college at Howard, she decided to study criminal justice and political science, which wasn't easy for her parents to understand at first. "My parents are Ethiopian, so they grew up with a lot of political instability. People who criticized the government weren't safe, so it's hard for them to see me advocating. It's really hard for us to see eye to eye sometimes."

During her junior year of high school, Elsa stumbled across the organization Zero Hour, a youth-led nonprofit environmental justice organization. This was the first time she noticed people talking about climate justice with a focus on the people who, according to Zero Hour's "Guiding Principles," are most affected by the climate crisis: "the Global South, People of Color,

Indigenous Peoples, Youth, People with Disabilities, Poor People, Women, Queer and Trans People, and People belonging to marginalized faiths."

Elsa was inspired to contact Zero Hour; she went on to become its national director of operations and logistics. In 2019 she planned a huge Zero Hour summit in Miami, Florida, to train 350 youth ambassadors to be climate leaders in their local communities.

All of Elsa's work—including organizing climate marches across the United States and serving on the board of Young Voices for the Planet, an organization that highlights kids from across the world—led to a lot of travel.

"At first it was, 'Elsa's going to Charlotte, North Carolina,' and my mom was scared," says Eta. "But then it was, 'Elsa's going to Puerto Rico, on the other side of the world!'" Eta adds, "Elsa knows how to take care of herself." But this doesn't stop her mom from fretting. "I get worried and nervous when she travels," Alemitu says. "I think, *What if something happens to Elsie?*" (Her mom calls her "Elsie.")

Before Elsa packed her bags for Italy, she spoke at the 2019 Climate Action Summit in Pittsburgh, Pennsylvania, where she said, "I'm 18 years old, and my future could be cut in half by a crisis I didn't create. This is very personal. I don't know what my future is going to look like. We are fighting for our lives."

Then Elsa tweeted a message to the world, knowing her mom is not on Twitter: "I booked a surprise trip to Rome for my mom!" That was the surprise up Elsa's sleeve.

In Rome, Elsa was one of 13 youth ambassadors speaking at a sustainability conference called YouthMundus, where she talked about "the transformational value of youth leadership in the climate movement, and the importance of taking care of ourselves and communities," Elsa says. "It's vital for us to have a space to communicate."

Elsa says she feels lifted up when she speaks alongside other young women who are working so hard to change the world. "Everywhere I go, I am surrounded by women who inspire me to go so much harder. I'm so blessed and privileged to even have the opportunity to sit in the same rooms as people who are actively changing the course of history, let alone be up on the stage and converse with them."

As Elsa's conference in Italy was about to end, back in North Carolina her siblings brought their mom to the airport and put her on a plane to Rome. "Oh yes, she surprised me! I never expected this in my life!" Alemitu says. "Italy was wonderful!"

Back home, Elsa didn't miss a beat before getting right back to work reminding everyone that the climate movement is connected to every social justice issue, including Black liberation, women's rights, gun regulation, and economic equity. For as long as she can remember, Elsa has been saying, "It's time for us to draw connections between the climate movement and every other movement. I'd like to see a cross-pollination of these."

In June 2020, after spending a day on back-to-back calls about Blackness and the climate, Elsa tweeted, "I think I've finally found where I fit into this movement."

Catarina Lorenzo

Born: March 30, 2007
Lives: Salvador, Brazil
Loves: Surfing
Instagram: @catarina_lorenzo
Pronouns: she/her/hers

Catarina Lorenzo loves the feeling of catching a wave and riding it as far as she can. She loves the challenge of balancing on her board during a big surf and floating on the crest of the wave.

Not long after Catarina took her first steps, she rode her first wave. She was only two years old when her dad brought her to the beach, plopped her on a surfboard, "and off I went!" she says.

Catarina lives in Bahia, a state in the northeastern part of Brazil that is known for its amazing waves and more than 4,500 miles of beautiful white sand beaches. In the summer, the waves can get up to 10 feet high. Her dad grew up surfing on these same beaches with his father and brothers.

Today, Catarina and her dad usually bike to the beach; he made a special handle on his bicycle to carry their surfboards. "My dad doesn't like to drive to the beach unless we're going far away," she says.

Bahia is located next to the largest coral reefs in the country. They're called the Abrolhos Archipelago. In Portuguese *abre olhos* means "open your eyes"—thus the name, because it's hard for ship captains to see their way as they try to navigate among the reefs.

"It's where humpback whales breed," Catarina says. There's even a shipwreck deep under the waters, she adds. This reef is one of richest and most vast coral reefs in the South Atlantic, home to more than 1,000 different species, from corals and fish to mollusks and crustaceans. Catarina has swum there her whole life. But every year, she has noticed something that deeply worries her: the coral reefs are turning white, which means they are dying.

Why are they dying? As the Earth's temperature rises every year, so does the temperature of the ocean. Until recently, coral reefs in Brazil seemed more resilient to warmer water, but in 2019 that changed. Scientists began to notice coral reefs dying off in Brazil unlike they'd ever seen.

That's why Catarina felt driven to speak up. She had to protect the ocean, the reefs, and the animals that depend on this ecosystem's balance to survive. Everything is connected, and reefs are among the most sensitive of all ecosystems to climate change.

Catarina lives in a region where mining companies dig for minerals such as iron, gold, and copper. This process damages the environment by eroding the land, which washes into the sea, carrying pollutants that in turn contaminate the oceans.

A couple of tragic accidents in this part of Brazil have polluted the water even more. In 2015 a local iron ore mine collapsed, causing tons of metal-contaminated slurry—a mixture of different substances and minerals mixed with water and oil—to slip into the water. The slurry contaminated the coral reefs as well as the river, which supplies water to the city. It also killed fish, which could no longer breathe because of low oxygen.

Then, four years later, in 2019, a giant oil tanker accidentally released 4,000 tons of oil into the Atlantic Ocean near the reefs. Thick clumps of smelly oil washed up on the shore, killing marine life and threatening coastal communities who make their living from tourists visiting. This oil spill was one of the largest environmental disasters ever in Brazil's history.

Today, oil continues to coat the reefs and beaches for hundreds of miles along the shore near Catarina's home. People are still trying to figure out who's responsible for this awful mess. No one has been punished or taken responsibility for the spill.

If the water is dirty, Catarina can't swim, so her mom, Caroline, keeps an ongoing list of polluted beaches to make sure her daughter surfs in clean water. On Instagram, Catarina regularly posts photos of her local beaches. She urges everyone to protect the oceans, because without them, we can't survive.

If Catarina sees oil on the shoreline, her mom contacts the local Guardiões do Litoral (Guardians of the Coast), a group of volunteers who are cleaning up the shoreline. This is not an easy job, because the oil clings to everything. Algae get covered with black sludge. Solid oil pellets float in the natural pools and dry up in the tide. "The people here deserve a prize because they stepped in to clean up the beaches," says Caroline about the volunteers who show up every week.

In 2019 the international law firm Hausfeld reached out to Catarina through the group Heirs to Our Oceans. The lawyers were filing a human rights complaint on behalf of young people who say that world leaders are failing to seriously address the climate crisis. They asked if Catarina wanted to speak up to the world. The case is called Children vs. Climate Crisis.

So, in September 2019, Catarina and her mom traveled to New York City to announce the climate complaint with 15 other young people from around the globe. They wanted to tell the world how their leaders are failing to act, even though they've known about the risks of climate change for decades. Everyone in the case was between 8 and 17 years old, including Swedish climate activist Greta Thunberg and, from India, one of the other Girl Warriors in this book, Ridhima Pandey.

"We will not permit them to take our future away," Catarina said. "They had the right to have their future; why don't we have the right to have our own?"

Catarina pointed out how Brazil has failed to cut its fossil fuel emissions. "If we don't act to stop the climate crisis, it will be the kids who pay the consequences," Catarina said to the UN Climate Action Summit. "I'm here to demand all the world leaders to listen to us and to help us stop climate change together."

The nonprofit Earthjustice filed this case with the UN Committee on the Rights of the Child. The organization submitted scientific research showing how specific countries have failed to act to reverse climate change. The goal of the petition is to use the international court system to put pressure on the most polluting countries to change.

Ridhima Pandey

Born: October 21, 2007
Lives: Haridwar, Uttarakhand, India
Loves: Dogs
Instagram: @ridhimapandeyy
Pronouns: she/her/hers

For as long as 12-year-old Ridhima can remember, she has loved animals. Especially dogs and cats.

When some stray dogs started to wander past her home in northern India, Ridhima would step outside to see them. The dogs looked at her with big, hungry eyes and panted with thirst. Ridhima decided to save bits of leftover food from her meals to feed the dogs. She also filled up bowls with water.

"It started with two dogs," say her parents, Vinita and Dinesh. "But during this lockdown, she's now feeding four or five dogs every day." The lockdown means sheltering in place during the COVID-19 pandemic. "Sometimes Ridhima also gives food and water to the cows because they aren't getting food anywhere else," her father says.

In Hinduism—a religion practiced by almost 80 percent of India's one billion people—cows are sacred, or holy, and many states do not allow cows to be killed for food. "Here in India, poor people raise cows for milk as their livelihood," Ridhima says. "They can't afford their [the cows'] food, so they can't stall-feed after milking in the morning. That's why they let the cows free for grazing." Cows often wander through the streets looking for food.

Maybe it shouldn't come as a big surprise that Ridhima loves animals so much. After all, her mom, Vinita, works in the forest department in their home state of Uttarakhand to protect trees and animals from poaching. And her dad, Dinesh, works for a nonprofit organization to protect wildlife in India.

"There's a tiger reserve near our home for animals to live. Elephants, tigers, other small animals sometimes come near the train tracks at night," Ridhima says. "So my dad is on a patrolling team, and the forest department's team patrols around there at night to prevent animals from getting hit and to keep them safe."

Ridhima and her brother, who's three years younger, like to stay up to wait for their dad to come home. They want to see if he snapped any photos of animals he saw.

Ridhima lives in a region of India called Haridwar, where the Ganges River flows from the Himalayas, a mountain range in northern India. In Hinduism, the Ganges is considered a sacred place, so people come from all over the country to visit and bathe there. For some people, this is their only water source to bathe or wash their clothes. But all her life, Ridhima has noticed how polluted the Ganges River is. Pipes from nearby buildings dump waste in the river, including sewage.

When she was six years old, the river flooded. Ridhima saw animals and trees swept away in the flood. Homes were destroyed. Some children were separated from their parents. "There is a shortage of water and electricity in my native place in the Nainital district, where my grandparents live," Ridhima says. "You had to wait two days to get fresh water. It was too much." Over the next few years, Ridhima and her parents talked about how little the government was doing to help people in their community get back on their feet to survive. That's why, when Ridhima was nine, she decided to speak up.

Her parents helped her file a petition, or a formal request addressed to the government, asking leaders of India to protect the environment. In her petition, she wrote, "India is one of the most vulnerable countries to be affected by climate change."

Unfortunately, the National Green Tribunal dismissed Ridhima's petition, saying the government was already doing enough. Today, her petition still sits in someone's office at the Supreme Court of India. "In the end, I didn't get justice," she says. "They dismissed it. We're seeing our future getting destroyed in front of our eyes."

However, "the story was published all over the world," adds Ridhima. "I was this nine-year-old girl who'd sued her government in India."

People started to hear about Ridhima in the news. One of those people was a lawyer at Hausfeld, a big law firm with offices in the United States and Europe. "What we all must do now is: talk less, act more," said Michael D. Hausfeld, the chair of Hausfeld. The law firm called Ridhima's family and explained that they were representing young people from around the world in a legal complaint to the UN Committee on the Rights of the Child. These young people were protesting five of the world's largest economies—Argentina, Brazil, France, Germany, and Turkey—for their role in the climate crisis. The lawyers wanted India to have a voice too.

"They asked my dad, 'Does your daughter want to be part of this?'" Ridhima says.

In September 2019, 11-year-old Ridhima and her father flew to New York, where they met activists from 12 different countries. The activists would be contributing to Hausfeld's case, called Children vs. Climate Crisis. Greta Thunberg from Sweden—who, at age 15, sparked the global movement for the planet when she stopped going to school to strike for the climate—was there, along with 15 other activists. They were all between the ages of ages 8 and 17. (One of them, Catarina Lorenzo from Brazil, is another Girl Warrior in this book.)

The activists each had a chance to address the UN representatives. "Namaste," Ridhima said into the microphone, a Sanskrit greeting that means "I bow to you." Then she said in English, "I am here because I want all the global leaders to do something to stop climate change. If it's not going to be stopped, it is going to harm our futures. So if we want to stop global warming, we have to do something now."

"I want a better future," she says. "I want to save my future. I want to save our future. I want to save the future of all the children and all people of future generations."

"It was really fun meeting kids from different countries to share stories and information," Ridhima reflects. "I got to make new friends and see how everyone else is tackling things. Everyone inspired me. They're all doing such hard work."

Vinita says that this trip to New York "was life changing because in India people are not very concerned about climate change or the environment. So after that UN summit, people started taking Ridhima's work seriously."

One of her biggest struggles back home is people's apathy, or lack of concern, about the climate. While her closest friends support her, Ridhima says many kids her age think she's just running around the world and raising her voice. "My best friends are happy for me," she says. "They join me on strikes. But some of my classmates think I'm just doing this so I can travel."

Even grown-ups have questioned Ridhima's actions. "Some adults tell me, 'You're so young. You shouldn't be doing this. You should just study,'" Ridhima says. "But even if it's a small change, my friends will benefit. It's like Greta says: 'No one is too small to make the change.'"

When she got home from the UN conference in the fall of 2019, people began to call Ridhima to ask her to speak. "I've been going to different schools and colleges all over the country to bring awareness," she says. "I talk about global warming and how it's affecting our health and future." Ridhima asks questions like "Do you know what's happening right now outside? Do you know that the air you're breathing is like you're inhaling five cigarettes a day?" she says. "I try to make them understand."

For example, Ridhima tells the kids to look around them and see how their environment is being destroyed. Do they see how polluted the sky is? What about the river? Did they notice the trees being cut down nearby?

"I talk about how we can all help, about what we can do," Ridhima says.

"I don't plan what I'm going to say. I don't speak from a script. I say what comes from my heart."

While sheltering in place during the COVID-19 pandemic, Ridhima started speaking up online. She stays connected to the activists from Children vs. Climate Crisis, and they choose themes to talk about on Instagram. "Today's theme was the forest, so I decided to post with the hashtag #SaveMangroves," Ridhima says, explaining that mangroves "are more than just an ordinary tree." Mangroves grow only in tropical areas. They are home to Bengal tigers, rhesus monkeys, estuarine crocodiles. Scientists call mangroves "super trees" because they store carbon and also reduce flooding and erosion from storms. And yet industries are "cutting down mangroves for mining and to build factories here," Ridhima says.

In an Instagram post, she wrote: "No forest, no future. India against deforestation. Save mangroves. My future, my life."

Isha Clarke

Born: January 16, 2003
Lives: Oakland, California, United States
Loves: Dancing
Instagram: @curlyqisha
Pronouns: she/her/hers

On February 22, 2019, teachers in Oakland, California, were on strike. Sixteen-year-old Isha Clarke didn't have school.

Isha was interning with a local group called Youth vs. Apocalypse; the group members headed to a climate crisis rally outside California senator Dianne Feinstein's office in San Francisco. During the rally, Isha connected with the Bay Area crew of another group, called Earth Guardians. They were headed to hand-deliver a letter they'd written to Senator Feinstein. In this letter, the Earth Guardians asked Feinstein if she would vote yes on the Green New Deal, a proposal that lays out a grand plan for leaders in the United States to tackle climate change. "It not only shows how the US can produce energy without emitting so many fossil fuels, it includes ways to build the economy in a just way in order to stop perpetuating destructive systems of oppression," Isha says.

That day, Feinstein invited a small group of mostly youth up to her office. But when they started to ask her questions, Feinstein grew defensive. She told them, "There's no way to pay for the Green New Deal."

"I've been doing this for thirty years," Feinstein said, referring to her time working in the Senate. "You come in here and say it has to be my way or the highway. I don't respond to that. . . . And I know what I'm doing. So, you know, maybe people should listen a little bit."

Isha *did* listen. She calmly addressed Feinstein and said, "I hear what you're saying, but we're the people who voted [for] you. You're supposed to listen to us. That's your job—"

"How old are you?" Feinstein interrupted Isha.

"I'm sixteen. I can't vote."

"Well, you didn't vote for me."

Isha recounts, "I told her, 'Our planet is dying. A bold and ambitious plan is needed!'"

Isha realized the conversation was not going in the right direction. "I could feel us getting away from humanity. I thought, *I'm a human being, you're a human being, let's talk.* I went up to her and I shook her hand and I said, 'Thank you for your time.'"

"She was getting really defensive and borderline disrespectful," Isha recalls. "But I stood up and I stood in my truth. I spoke truth to power."

On her way home on the train, one of Isha's teachers messaged her that she was proud. Isha didn't know what her teacher was talking about. "Have you seen Twitter?" her teacher asked. Within an hour, the interaction between Isha and Feinstein had gone viral. "I had no idea what a big deal this would be." The story eventually would be picked up by the *Guardian*, Democracy Now!, *Teen Vogue, Grist, Mercury News*, and more. Within a year, more than 10 million viewers would see the two-minute clip.

Isha's head was spinning after meeting Feinstein. On the one hand, she felt defeated because Feinstein had not acknowledged the severity of the climate crisis for youth. But Isha was also energized. "This day changed the course for climate justice. It was a pivotal moment in my life!" Isha wanted to speak the truth. And she wanted to make sure she was heard.

In addition to her activism, Isha also dances eight hours a week at Destiny Arts Center, a nonprofit in Oakland for youth ages 3–18. The name Destiny stands for "De-Escalation Skills Training Inspiring Nonviolence in

Youth." "I went to dance class that afternoon after meeting Feinstein, and I started getting all of these calls from the media." Isha had to step out of class and sit in her teacher's office to answer questions from reporters.

Isha is a serious student. She skipped first grade, and as a high school freshman she started taking classes at Laney College, a community college in Oakland. "It's really hard sometimes to try to do everything and balance all of my commitments," Isha says. "Dance is my therapy. I honestly believe that if I didn't have Destiny, I'd go insane."

Yet Isha's experience with Feinstein was not the first time she'd spoken up to a prominent, successful grown-up in public. When Isha was a freshman in high school, she and a group of Bay Area youth went to deliver a message to Phil Tagami, an investor who was trying to build a coal terminal in West Oakland, a predominantly Black community that already suffers from severe health issues. "We told him, 'You can't bring the coal here.'"

Tagami dismissed the kids, not unlike the way Senator Feinstein did. "I remember standing there and feeling disgusted," Isha says. "So I spoke up."

"This coal is going to poison us," she told him. Isha and her friends told Tagami that their asthma would get worse if he burned coal.

"We need to stop shipping and burning coal to have a chance of slowing this climate crisis," Isha wrote in a piece for the *East Bay Express*. "This coal terminal is racist and poisonous. It's up to us—people on the frontlines—to make sure that it doesn't come into our community."

"In that moment, I found my power," Isha says. "I understood that I was supposed to do this."

Isha has since become a vocal climate activist in the Bay Area, energizing crowds at rallies and speaking to large audiences who've come to hear her. She has many mentors, including Malik Edwards, a former Black Panther in Oakland.

"The Black Panthers are one of my biggest political influences, because they're a radical Black revolutionary group from Oakland," Isha says. "We can't actually meet our goal of reversing climate change if we don't acknowledge the systems of oppression—like racism, White supremacy, and greed—that led us to the climate crisis."

Isha also finds inspiration at home. Her father is Black, and her mom is Jewish. "I'm really close to my mom. She has literally turned into my mom-a-ger!" Isha adds, "My mom *really* knows me, and she's always there, no matter what. She helps me get through things." The day after the Feinstein confrontation—on Isha's 17th birthday—her mom flew to Los Angeles with Isha, who'd been invited to speak to a big group of educators about the climate crisis.

Isha's Mom, Mara Tobis, describes her daughter as "fierce." "Isha is so courageous and powerful," Mara says. "She's also like a sponge, always wanting to learn more."

In June 2020, Isha organized friends and other activists into a new group: Black Youth for the People's Liberation. For Juneteenth, observed on June 19 to commemorate the end of slavery in the United States, Isha led "BY4PL" through West Oakland, with everyone wearing masks as a safety measure against COVID-19.

Into the mic, Isha spoke to a huge crowd about systemic racism. "We must dismantle all of these systems in order to be free! Our country and our world have been built upon a faulty foundation!"

In 2020, Isha won a Diller Teen Tikkun Olam Award from the Helen Diller Family Foundation for bringing to light climate injustices that affect low-income communities of color. The award will help support Isha's tuition when she to heads to Howard University in Washington, DC.

In the meantime, Isha is organizing a strike for climate justice. "Whatever I'm working on, I want it to be around the idea of true intersectionality," she says. "The causes of climate change are these systems of oppression: White supremacy, colonialism, and capitalism. They are unsustainable and destructive. Climate justice is about dismantling these systems of oppression. At the end of the day, we're fighting for collective liberation."

Hannah Testa

Born: October 19, 2002
Lives: Cumming, Georgia, United States
Loves: Her golden retriever, Butterball
Instagram: @hannah4change
Pronouns: she/her/hers

Everywhere she looks, Hannah sees plastic, like in the trash cans at her school. The cafeteria uses Styrofoam trays, and her district buys 50,000 plastic straws every year.

"The average American uses 500 plastic bags each year, and the US uses 500 million plastic straws each day that end up polluting our oceans," she says.

Hannah had to start somewhere. That place was home, in Georgia.

Hannah was 13 when she contacted two Georgia state senators to help her to educate people in her state about the plastic pollution crisis. "By 2050, plastics in the ocean will outweigh the fish," she told them. "Plastic pollution kills countless birds and sea animals, contributes to coral reef decline, and shows up in our food chain."

On February 15, 2017, Hannah stood in front of the Georgia State Senate, where the state's elected leaders make laws and decisions. She urged her state senators to do something about plastic pollution. "Not only does plastic end up on our streets, streams, and oceans," Hanna told them, "it also affects 600 species of marine life, through ingestion and entanglement, often killing them."

Thanks to Hannah, her state designated that day—February 15—as Plastic Pollution Awareness Day, the first event of its kind to urge citizens and businesses to commit to one day of avoiding single-use plastics.

"I don't have a right to vote yet," Hannah said then. "But I have a voice."

When she was younger, Hannah's parents helped her draft her speeches. Now she writes them on her own. Sometimes her little brother, Adam, sits and listens as her audience.

Hannah's grandparents are from the island of Mauritius in the Indian Ocean. Hannah's mom, Farida, grew up in London, where her family always brought their own bags to the store, so she carried this practice with her when she raised her own kids. Hannah noticed that her mom never took a plastic bag home, even if her parents didn't really talk about it.

One day, Hannah asked her mom why other people didn't carry their own bags to the store like their family did. "Mama, no one cares about our planet but us," she told Farida one day. "We're the only ones in the store with a reusable bag."

Farida, a preschool teacher, wanted to support her daughter's curiosity about the world. Together they started an organic garden in their backyard and grew tomato plants for Hannah's class. Hannah told her friends what natural resources were and why they had to be protected. She reminded other kids to turn off lights when they left the room and to shut off the faucet after washing their hands.

Her teachers noticed Hannah's new activism, and in elementary school, her community honored her with her first advocate award. Hannah has been unstoppable since.

When Hannah was 14, she walked into a Ted's Montana Grill, a chain restaurant that's co-owned by Ted Turner, an American businessman and the founder of the cable news channel CNN. She asked to speak to the manager because she wanted to thank the restaurant for using paper straws. This conversation led to an introduction to Turner, which in turn led to meeting some of his family members who run environmental organizations. Today, Hannah works with Ted Turner's daughter and grandson for the Captain Planet Foundation, where she talks to big audiences about sustainability.

"I still get really nervous when I speak," Hannah says. "That really doesn't go away. But I think being nervous shows that you care. I want to make an impact."

Some of her friends who are also activists have given her tips before she goes on stage, like how to shake out her hands and legs when she's waiting behind the curtain. When it's time to get up to the podium, Hannah knows people need to listen.

Hannah's mom describes her as "confident, but also humble. She treats everyone, including animals, like she would want to be treated. Hannah's goal continues to be: show others how simple changes can greatly reduce our plastic footprint on the Earth."

It's not always easy. In her sophomore year, another classmate harassed Hannah at school. "He was trying to bring me down." But she turned to her friends for support. "Don't let him take away your worth," one of her girlfriends reminded her.

Hannah celebrated her 16th birthday midflight on her way to the international youth festival Youthfull in Bahrain, a country in the Persian Gulf. The plane took off, and from her window seat next to her mom, she looked down at the Atlantic Ocean. She thought about the enormous pockets of plastic trapped in the currents. She thought about all the marine animals struggling to survive.

When Hannah got on stage in front of thousands of people, her hands shook. She was the youngest speaker there. She took a deep breath and said into the microphone, "Eight million tons of plastic enter our oceans every year, poisoning them." Her steady voice filled the theater. "We have to stop this."

Today, she is a junior in high school in Cumming, Georgia, a suburb 40 minutes outside Atlanta. Hannah is starting to see changes in her community, such as paper straws in restaurants. Every day, between finishing homework and planning her next trip, Hannah writes speeches, jumps on conference calls, and travels to events. She even wrote a book, *Taking on the Plastics Crisis*, which was published in October 2020 by Penguin Random House.

She's also vegan. Her parents and brother decided not to eat meat anymore, either. "Hannah has made me a better human being," her mom says.

Haven Coleman

Born: March 29, 2006
Lives: Denver, Colorado, United States
Loves: Laughing
Instagram: @climateactivist
Pronouns: she/her/hers

Haven was 11 years old when she asked her mom to drive her to a town hall meeting in Denver, where her district's congressional representative was going to speak.

Haven, who loves science and proudly calls herself "a nerd," had been reading the news every day, so she knew that the congressman, Doug Lamborn, didn't believe that humans cause climate change. That's why Haven was determined to speak to Representative Lamborn in person. He had to start reading the science. He had to know the facts.

When it was time for Lamborn to take questions from the large crowd in Denver, Haven took the microphone and told her congressman that humans were indeed causing climate change. She also told him it was time for leaders "to pursue renewable energy," which means power that comes from nonpolluting sources found in nature, such as sunlight, wind, rain, tides, and waves.

Haven went on to explain why solar and wind energy are both clean and safe, and why these new industries could create lots of jobs in their state.

Haven then invited Lamborn to her science class the following week for a presentation she was planning about the climate crisis.

Although her congressman never showed up to her fifth grade class, this didn't stop Haven. Her mom, Nicole, filmed her leading a 15-minute science lesson and then sent it to Congressman Lamborn's office. He never responded, although "in an email his aide said he would show the video to the congressman," Haven says.

Haven first learned about the climate at age 10, when her social studies teacher taught a lesson on deforestation. That was when she learned that her favorite animal, the sloth, was losing its home. She was devastated to hear how sloths were suffering. She began to understand how urgent things were.

Haven asked her mom to sign her up for a course with the Climate Reality Project, an organization started by former US vice president Al Gore. Haven wanted to learn how to give public talks about the harmful effects of climate change. That weekend, she was one of the youngest people at the training!

"I *had* to do something!" Haven says. "It's been nonstop climate activism since." Haven was driven to speak up for animals, for people, and for future generations because, she says, "if adults aren't going to do anything, who will?"

"The kids!" she replies, answering her own question.

At age 11, Haven went to another town hall to speak to Colorado senator Cory Gardner. She urged him to form a special group in the Senate that will find climate solutions. "If all you need is more information, I can come visit the energy committee and do a PowerPoint for you," Haven said.

Around this time, Haven also heard about climate activist Greta Thunberg, the then-15-year-old who'd started to leave school on Fridays to strike outside the Riksdag, the Swedish parliament. Haven wanted to follow Greta's lead in her own state, so she wrote Greta's words in English on a sign: SCHOOL STRIKE FOR CLIMATE. Her mom agreed to drive her to downtown Denver every Friday at lunch to strike.

It was not easy. Trying to get adults to change their behavior is like potty-training a kid, Haven says. "It feels like we're trying to push them to use the toilet, the way parents push their toddlers. It's really stressful!" Some days, she feels very scared and worried. Other days, she feels on fire because she has to wake people up.

By the time she was in eighth grade, Haven's days began with checking her email and social media accounts. "My mom helps me stay organized, because I have dyslexia and dysgraphia," which makes writing difficult, Haven says. "My mom goes through my inbox, finds the most important emails, and reads them out loud to me."

"My mom also helps me stay calm and spell-checks my work," Haven says. "She's there for me. She drives me places and accompanies me to events. She also motivates me and helps me be happy."

Haven's mom says it's challenging to manage everything. "I spend an enormous amount of time trying to juggle our family life with managing the spontaneous trips, interviews, and opportunities she has, and helping her talk through the very adult decisions she has to work though daily. We also spend a lot of time dealing with the emotional trauma this work puts her through."

In 2019, Haven was thrilled to go to New York City to strike with Greta Thunberg. She traveled with her SCHOOL STRIKE FOR CLIMATE poster from home, and when her poster accidentally got caught in the door of the New York City subway—"and looked beat up!"—she refused to let it bring her down.

Her sense of humor lifts her up on hard days. "Joy is an act of resistance," she says. "We can't be serious all the time, or we go somewhere so dark we have no energy to continue the fight."

After coming back home from New York City, Haven got a message from Greta that she might visit Colorado as she traveled across the United States. Sure enough, a few weeks later, Greta confirmed that she'd be joining 13-year-old Haven for her climate strike in Denver. Haven had a week and a half to get ready for Greta's arrival. "Me and my activism community made it happen fast, with little money and little time, but it was awesome!" Haven says.

For more than 40 weeks before this, Haven had been solo—or with a handful of people—on her Friday strikes, so Greta's arrival was a big deal. Haven did her best to organize the rally downtown, but she didn't have a lot of details, other than knowing that she'd need to provide meals and security for Greta.

Haven was thrilled to see such a huge crowd waiting to hear Greta, but she didn't appreciate the media who kept pushing people aside to take photos next to Greta. "I blocked the reporter with my sign to block his camera, because she didn't want any more photos," Haven says. "He said 'Move it' and pushed my sign. I pushed my sign back at him and said, 'She doesn't want pictures,' and we just kept going. It was a huge crowd following us and trying to take photos."

"I take my guard job seriously," Haven says, half joking; although Greta had real guards present, Haven felt compelled to protect her friend. "I wanted to make sure that Greta was safe. My dad, who's a pretty big guy, helped her walk through the crowd."

Before Haven and Greta spoke on stage, they managed to find a quiet place to get a bite to eat and chat. "We talked about different types of snow and all the ways you can describe snow in English and Swedish. I liked talking to her. I liked seeing everybody there."

But a few thousand people were waiting; it was time for Haven and Greta to get on stage. Haven's heart pounded hard as she approached the microphone and faced the crowd. "You need to understand that we're striking to protect our future," Haven told the crowd at Civic Center Park in a very clear, confident voice. "We have a right to a livable planet. Our hard work does not absolve you of action. We cannot do it all. You need to step up and step in."

"This is real hope, what we're seeing right now," Greta said. "This is the hope—the people."

The year 2019 was a big one for Haven: She came out as gay to her family and to the world. Magazines such as *Out* and the *Advocate* profiled her story.

The next spring, Haven was all set to travel to Austin, Texas, where she'd been invited to speak at South by Southwest, a 10-day conference where hundreds of thousands of people flock to listen to speakers and music, watch films, and learn. Unfortunately, due to the COVID-19 pandemic, the conference was canceled. "It is very disappointing since I'd worked so hard on my talks," Haven says. "Plus I had planned to meet some pretty cool people there. Maybe I will get another chance to go another year." She'd planned to speak about "education and climate, with girl empowerment in the mix," Haven says.

Not surprisingly, Haven would have been the youngest speaker on stage.

In the meantime, Haven continues to speak up for the climate from her home in Colorado, where she celebrated her recent birthday with the theme "QuaranTEEN for FourTEEN!"

Lilly Platt

Born: April 18, 2008
Lives: Zeist, the Netherlands
Loves: Painting with watercolors
Instagram: @lillys_plastic_pickup
Pronouns: she/her/hers

When Lilly was seven years old, she and her grandpa started to take walks together around her town in the middle of the Netherlands so she could learn Dutch. As it turned out, they did much more than that.

That's because, not too long into their walks together, Lilly started to notice all of the trash on the ground. Grandpa Jim figured this would be a good way to teach Lilly how to count: they'd count every piece of trash together. Counting in Dutch isn't easy, because when you say a double digit, the second number comes first: 1 is *een* and 20 is *twintig*, but 21 is *eenentwintig*—"one and twenty."

"It was a way for me to practice," Lilly says. "One day, we tried to guess how many pieces we could count on our 10-minute walk. We counted 91 pieces!"

"Grandpa told me that anything that falls on the ground would somehow make its way to the plastic soup," Lilly says. The plastic soup is an enormous garbage patch that's swirling around the center of the Pacific Ocean. It's not just large pieces of single-use plastic; it includes small pieces of plastic that fall apart and get eaten by marine life. "It could take a day, a week, a month, or a whole year, but plastic will make its way to the ocean. That was the moment I decided to pick up every bit of plastic I found." Thus Lilly's Plastic Pickup was born.

One day, Lilly and Grandpa Jim found a 20-year-old empty chip bag someone had tossed. Another day, they picked up a plastic bottle that was more than a decade old. Back home, Lilly lined up every piece of trash, categorizing them into groups such as plastic bottles, fast food containers, wrappers, and bags.

Every day, their walks got longer as they picked up all of the rubbish people had tossed. Lilly calls trash *rubbish* in English. Whenever she says the word, she punches the air with her fist. In the Netherlands, the word for garbage is *zwerfafval*, which translates to "stray rubbish."

Ever since Lilly and Grandpa Jim, who's a geologist, picked up that first piece of trash, her life has not been the same. Lilly's goal is to make the environment clean and safe for all future generations, and she does this by setting an example in her own life.

Lilly's mom, Eleanor, started to take photos of all the trash they collected. She posted them on Instagram, and that's how people all over the world started to notice this young girl who was cleaning up her corner of the Earth. Lilly was invited to the World Youth Forum in Egypt, where she was the youngest speaker. At age nine, she got invited to Norway for the Plastic Whale Coastal Clean-Up and Conference, which took place in memory of a Cuvier's beaked whale that died on the Norwegian coast with its stomach full of more than 30 plastic bags. Lilly met environmentalists from around the world to talk about the growing problem of plastic waste and how to protect our coastlines.

She celebrated her 10th birthday with Lilly's Global Cleanup Day, a plan to get people all around the world to pick up trash with her. In the end, people in 27 countries cleaned up rubbish in their communities. She says it was the best present she could've asked for.

Lilly would love to see a ban on plastic bags in stores around the world and a ban on balloon releases at big events. She also wants all schools to educate young people about the climate crisis and plastic pollution.

Thanks to a connection between Grandpa Jim and a mutual friend of Jane Goodall, who is the world's expert on chimpanzees, Lilly has met the famous anthropologist a few times. Jane Goodall asked Lilly to work with her on a project to reduce plastic pollution.

Today, at age 12, Lilly records videos for Instagram in her bedroom every week. She records all of her videos spontaneously. "I don't write anything down," she says. "I just think it and say it." She pleads with people to stop throwing their garbage on the ground. "There's no away! Plastic stays!" Lilly said in one video, her hands moving in the air as if she were performing a magic trick. "Remember to pick up your rubbish, kids!" She jumped close to the screen with her big, imploring eyes behind her glasses. Lilly often ends her greetings with: "Have a plastic-free day!"

"She sits in her room upstairs, and we can hear her talking," says Eleanor, who's a Montessori teacher. "I believe all children have absorbent minds. Whenever Lilly has been interested in anything, we've tried to find books to encourage her to learn." By the time Lilly was 12, she'd transitioned to homeschooling.

Unfortunately, also around this time, internet trolls started to target Lilly and other young activists with online abuse. One morning, after Lilly tweeted about deforestation, a swarm of disturbing photos and inappropriate messages started flooding her Twitter feed. Her mom asked Lilly's followers to flag the posts for removal, and they did.

When Lilly isn't traveling or speaking about the environment, she loves to read, paint, and play with her cats and dogs. She and her family have two greyhounds (Poppy and Olea), three cats (Julius and Sylvester, who are 18 years old, and Pookie, who is 7), and two turtles (Binky and Sparky). Their family's recent addition is a pug named Mochi, "who was Lilly's heart's desire," Eleanor says.

Lilly and her brother, John Henry, who's 15 years older than she, are big Harry Potter fans. Lilly especially loves to paint Harry Potter characters. She taught herself how to draw, and by the time she was 12, Lilly had filled 60 journals with her sketches and watercolors. "I always bring my art supplies and journal where I go, sketch whenever I get the chance."

Of course, she spends as much time with Grandpa Jim as she can. "He is a living tree of knowledge," Lilly says. "He's the one who told me that all of this trash would go into the ocean one day, by way of rain or wind or the drains, and because plastic isn't biodegradable, he explained to me that it just stays there and breaks down into microplastics. The plankton eat the microplastic, and the fish eat the plankton, and that's how the plastic gets into us."

He explains every kind of rock and mineral to Lilly, and sometimes they go searching for fossils in stones. Grandpa Jim turned 80 just before the COVID-19 pandemic broke out.

At first, Lilly's mom thought the lockdown would last only a few weeks, so she sent Lilly to stay with Grandpa Jim. "I work three days from home without seeing anyone, so I'm able to spend four days a week with Lilly and Grandpa. It has all worked out well."

Grandpa Jim helps Lilly with her homework every day, and they go on walks together. After the COVID-19 outbreak, Lilly and her grandpa stopped picking up trash, because Grandpa Jim needs to stay healthy and safe.

"He's my champion," Lilly says about her grandpa. "He's traveled all around the world, and he knows so much about nature. He's one of the best cooks in the entire galaxy!" When Lilly writes about Grandpa Jim online, she usually tags him #bestfriendsforlife.

Ayisha Siddiqa

Born: February 8, 1999
Lives: Coney Island, New York, United States
Loves: Reading and writing poetry
Instagram: @ayisha_sid
Pronouns: she/her/hers

On a Wednesday morning in October 2019, a crowd gathered at Wall Street in downtown New York City, where Ayisha Siddiqa, a 20-year-old student at Hunter College, was speaking into a megaphone.

"I came to the United States from Pakistan when I was six years old," Ayisha says. "My family lived for thousands of years on rural land by the Chenab River." Ayisha describes Jhang, the region of Punjab where she's from: "There was extreme poverty. The river has been massively polluted. Water sources are very difficult to filter and clean. The dirty water has caused so many illnesses, including polio and malaria."

"Pakistan contributes less than 1 percent of the global greenhouse gas emissions but is the eighth most affected country from climate change," Ayisha says. "But in competition with the rest of the industrialized world, Pakistan is forced to rely on nonrenewable energy because renewable energy has been made so expensive for the Global South. It is a lose-lose situation. If you are a poor country and want to economically compete with the rest of the world, you have to rely on harmful energy; otherwise you risk extreme hunger and societal collapse."

The Wall Street crowd gathered to watch the protest that Ayisha had helped organize. It's also likely that some of these Wall Street people worked with or for fossil fuel investors.

Ayisha wanted people to understand how the pollution and environmental devastation in Pakistan is very similar to what's happening today in their community in New York. She wanted them to see that people of color around the world are the most vulnerable to the climate crisis. These are the same people who have lost their land to the oil industry and who have gotten sick from water polluted by industrial waste. These are also the people who have no seats at the table when it's time to discuss real solutions to the climate crisis.

That Wednesday morning, after leading the rally at Wall Street, Ayisha took the subway six miles uptown to Hunter College, where she's studying political science and creative writing. "I had a midterm, so after I led the action, I ran back to school!" Ayisha says. Then, following a full day of classes, she headed across Central Park to a basement where a group of students meets every Wednesday evening for two hours. "A lot of world-changing stuff has occurred in this basement!" Ayisha laughs. This basement is home to the New York Society for Ethical Culture. It's where the NYC Climate Action Alliance and many other climate groups plan, organize, and mobilize.

Ayisha began to organize in the climate movement when she was 18, and one year later, she joined the international group Extinction Rebellion, or XR for short. XR describes itself as a leaderless group that uses nonviolent direct action to call attention to climate change and biodiversity loss.

Ayisha couldn't help but notice the lack of college students at the XR meetings. Maybe they were nervous about speaking up or striking, she wondered. She understood their apprehension. "If you cut school, you could be hurting yourself and your tuition," she says. "Also, it doesn't seem appropriate to strike from school when you are paying to go to that school." That was how the idea for Extinction Rebellion Universities was born, although Ayisha shies away from calling herself a founder. As more students at colleges and universities across the globe realize that their own schools are invested in fossil fuel companies—making money off practices that are harming the planet—they are rising up to demand the schools *divest*, or give up these investments.

XR Universities merged with NYC Climate Action Alliance, Ayisha says. "The coalition mainly consisted of youth from high school and middle school, but there was a lack of college students, particularly those engaging in direct action." The group talked about places they could occupy, or take over, as part of a strike. "At a university you can occupy a president's office or a library," Ayisha says. "The impact is direct. You can target very specific people with power. Your demands can be specific. For example, you can say, 'Tell the truth: How much do you invest in the fossil fuel industry? How much money are you taking? Are you involved second-hand in coal mines? Or in oil drilling?'"

Today, 30 autonomous chapters of XR Universities meet across the United States. "XR Uni is a hub that offers universities the training needed to take direct action and access to XR branding/content," Ayisha says.

Ayisha saw firsthand how direct action could create change. So, at age 20, she stepped up to co-organize New York City's climate strike on September 20, 2019.

In the same basement of the New York Society for Ethical Culture, Ayisha and her peers planned the event, secured permits to strike, contacted the media, and lobbied Congress. On September 20, more than 250,000 people converged in the streets to stand up for the climate and their future.

Ayisha lives with her parents, two sisters, and a brother on Coney Island, two blocks from the shore, where "lots of immigrants and Black and Brown people live," she says. Families there are still recovering from Hurricane Sandy, a deadly and destructive hurricane that hit her neighborhood in 2012.

Ayisha's sister Hafsa Fatima describes her as "resilient, thoughtful, and bold." Hafsa Fatima, who is two years younger, recalls going to one of the rallies that Ayisha led in Central Park. "I saw her lead a group of people, with such a diversity of ages and races," Hafsa Fatima says. "At home, I hear her having her meetings every day with climate activists from all around the world; sometimes it's 3:00 AM, and sometimes it's bright and early at 6:00 AM. I admire her ability to prioritize her activism even if she has an exam the very next day."

Ayisha is on the phone at all hours, making international calls to activists around the world. "I have to stay up late to make time zones align," she says. "Often we get on the phone at 2:00 to 4:00 AM to go over weekly progress reports. We prefer to talk on the phone, rather than texting. It [texting] leaves so much room for miscommunication. Communication is key! A small misunderstanding can arise and people get unmotivated."

In early 2020, Ayisha cofounded Polluters Out with two other activists—Isabella Fallahi, another Girl Warrior in this book, who's from Indiana, and Helena Gualinga, an Indigenous environmental and human rights activist from the Kichwa community of Sarayaku in Pastaza, Ecuador. Polluters Out is a global youth movement that calls out the fossil fuel industry. The trio created it as a reaction to the 2019 UN Climate Change Conference (COP25).

During the UN conference in Madrid, Spain, they had seen firsthand how the fossil fuel industry influenced international climate decisions. For example, two of the largest electric utility companies in the world, Endesa and Iberdrola, paid more than $2 million for "platinum sponsorship" status. This gave these companies seats at the table during climate talks, while the people most affected by the climate crisis were left out of the conversations.

Ayisha and the cofounders of Polluters Out say it is time for the UN to stop accepting polluted money. "For the past 20 years, they've accomplished nothing," Ayisha says. She points out that way back in 1992, the UN first told countries they had to reduce their greenhouse gas emissions by 5 percent between the years 1990 and 2010. But the agreement was nonbinding, meaning nations such as the United States did not have any obligation to cut their emissions.

Polluters Out officially launched in January 2020. Every week, Ayisha hosts international calls with more than 80 activists from all over the world: Canada, Germany, the United Kingdom, Australia, Costa Rica, Morocco, India, Kenya, and American Samoa.

The lack of sleep can lead to burnout and anxiety, Ayisha says. "I usually go to sleep around 3:00 AM, then wake up at 9:00 AM to go to classes. If I'm not in class, I'm meeting with a journalist or the team." Sometimes she logs offline to play her guitar or to read poetry. She's a big fan of Mary Oliver.

Polluters Out had planned an International Day of Action for March 20, 2020, to name the culprits in the fossil fuel industry, meaning the people and companies who are responsible for global warming. "The youth are calling on the UNFCCC [the United Nations Framework Convention on Climate Change], world governments, banks, universities, and corporations to divest and separate themselves from the controlling influence of the fossil fuel industry so that the world can begin to see the implementation of real solutions, not loopholes," the organizers said in their press release. But as COVID-19 spread, assembling in person wasn't safe, so Polluters Out moved the event online for a global protest with the hashtag #PollutersOut. The strike was big and bold.

"Climate justice is about people," Ayisha said in an Instagram live chat in May 2020. "If people are not making this connection, if they don't have this understanding, then they've chosen to be oblivious."

In spring 2020 the University of California system became the largest university system in the United States to divest fully from fossil fuels. And that summer, Harvard University alumni voted to fill three positions on the school's Board of Overseers with candidates who promised to push for divestment.

Today, Ayisha is working on a new project called Fossil Fuel University, "exclusively designed for youth activists on the front lines, including the team of Polluters Out, to network." A team of "adult mentors who have been in the climate fight for decades" have signed on to support the activists as they learn how to lobby, organize, and put pressure on the fossil fuel industry. "Education in terms of the climate crisis is not as simple as reading the IPCC [Intergovernmental Panel on Climate Change] reports," Ayisha says. "It takes years to accumulate a comprehensive understanding of the intricacies of the crisis. That's why Polluters Out wanted to give our own team the tools necessary to take on the fossil fuel industry forthright."

World of Me Maria

Melati and Isabel Wijsen

Melati Born: December 19, 2000
Isabel Born: November 6, 2002
Live: Bali, Indonesia
Love: Each other and the beach
Instagram: @melatiwijsen,
@isabel.wijsen, @byebyeplasticbags,
and @youthtopia.world
Melati's Pronouns: she/her/hers
Isabel's Pronouns: she/her/hers

Melati and her younger sister, Isabel, have loved the beach since they were babies, when their parents first started bringing them to the shore.

Their mother, Elvira, who's Dutch, fell in love with their father, Eko, who's Javanese, while working on a boat in Indonesia, where they've raised their two daughters in the sunshine and sand, swimming and snorkeling.

"We were best friends growing up, and we still are," Melati says about her relationship with her sister, whom she calls Bel. "My parents fostered this friendship between us." She adds, "Sure, we're also teenagers, so sometimes we clash over different views, and that's normal. Otherwise it would be too many rainbows!"

Whenever they went to the beach as little kids, they picked up garbage on the shore. Plastic bottles and cups have littered the sand for as long as they can remember. If the sisters went out to swim, they had to wade through plastic. Even on hikes through the local rice fields, they had to step over trash. Whenever they picked up plastic bags from the ground, they read the names from local stores and knew these bags had come from right next door. Indonesia dumps more plastic into the ocean than any other country except China.

When Melati was 10 and Bel was 8, they realized the trash in their community wasn't going away. "Almost all plastic bags in Bali end up in our drains, and then in our rivers, and then in our ocean," Melati says. "Those that don't make it to the ocean are either burned or littered."

The rainy season made the cycle even worse. Things got so bad at one point that soldiers were deployed to fish Styrofoam food containers and plastic bags out of the water. Part of the challenge was that landfills were so full they couldn't hold any more waste.

Growing up, Melati's parents "always took us very seriously," she says. "Family dinners were not just about 'How was your day?' We had discussions. We dove deep into bigger issues." With their parents' support, the sisters started to organize group cleanups in the community. It was a start, but the plastic problem was not going away. They wanted to do more. Could 8- and 10-year-old girls really make a difference? Melati and Bel decided together that they would try. Their mom helped them found a nonprofit organization called Bye Bye Plastic Bags so they could empower people to say no to single-use plastic in Bali.

Melati describes her mom as "my mentor. She gets stuff done. She gets me to pick up my boots and go, go, go."

Melati and Bel started an online petition to ban single-use plastic bags from retailers in Bali. Word quickly spread, and they collected thousands of signatures in one day. They also organized massive beach cleanups, provided more than 35,000 alternative bags to local people, and lobbied with local and national governments. They even went on a hunger strike to get their leaders' attention.

In the span of a few years, the sisters gave four TED Talks. In their talk in 2016, 13-year-old Bel told the audience that, in a single day, her country generates an amount of trash that could be piled as high as a 14-story building. In fact, Indonesia is one of the world's worst contributors of plastic pollution into the ocean, according to the World Economic Forum.

Magazines and news sites all over the world—including *Forbes* and *Time*—included the sisters in lists of the world's most influential teenagers. Today, Bye Bye Plastic Bags has become an international movement to eliminate plastic bags, with close to 50 chapters around the world. Melati and Bel credit their school, Green School Bali, for encouraging them to become international leaders.

At the end of 2019, the sisters got some big, exciting news: Bali's governor had announced a law banning single-use plastic. "Don't ever let anyone tell you that you're too young or you won't understand," Bel says. "We're not telling you it's going to be easy. We're telling you it's going to be worth it."

In her free time, Bel loves to study, dance, and perform. She loves school. Melati graduated high school a year early, in 2018, and says, "I decided university wasn't really for me, at least for now."

In 2020, Melati was hard at work on a new global project called Youthtopia, an idea she first had when she was 15 years old. "It's about bringing youth together to connect and generate ideas and solutions that benefit the world's environment and humanity," she says. Youthtopia empowers youth at home to transform the world to make it a better place for all. Anyone can register to take online classes and workshops.

On evenings, Melati loves to slip off her flip-flops and walk down to the beach, a stone's throw away from her home. Sometimes her sister joins her. After working long hours every day, they love to look at the moon, especially when it's full. "A full moon is a good time to reflect," Melati says. On a recent full moon, she sank her toes into the sand, breathed in the salty air, and reflected on the past 10 years in her life, a mix of inspiring, challenging, and especially exhilarating experiences.

Kallan Benson

Born: February 17, 2004
Lives: Crownsville, Maryland, United States
Loves: Playing the cello
Instagram: @releaf4us
Pronouns: she/her/hers

Kallan Benson's mom refers to her daughter as a "girl in the wings."

When you're "in the wings," you're ready to do something. In theater, "in the wings" means you're ready to go on stage.

Kallan was nine years old when she first waited in the wings, as a volunteer at her local community theater outside Washington, DC. "People assumed that she aspired to the stage, like many little girls, but she loved serving as an usher," her mom, Kimberly, says.

For the next two years, Kallan stood ready to help people find their seats, until, at age 11, she was thrilled to be tall enough to volunteer as a spotlight operator. For the next few years, she waited in the wings to light every production.

"Center stage never held much appeal to her," Kimberly says. "She preferred to cast others in favorable light: bathing them in color, softening the shadows, bringing out their brilliance, helping them find a place to shine."

During this time, Kallan's mom—a marine scientist who used to work for the National Oceanic and Atmospheric Administration—took Kallan and her brother, Reece, who's 17 months younger, to New York City. There they participated in the People's Climate March with a group of their fellow Quakers. Quakers are a Christian group, also known as the Religious Society of Friends, who follow six values called SPICES, which stands for: simplicity, peace, integrity, community, equality, and stewardship. Quakers, or Friends, have a long history of social activism. They've worked to free enslaved people and abolish slavery. They've been involved in civil rights, women's rights, and voting rights movements. They've marched to end war and stand for equality.

Kallan's first national climate march marked the beginning of her activism. Being homeschooled also influenced her. "I've been going to the Smithsonian since I can remember," says Kallan, referring to the 9 research centers, 19 museums, and 21 libraries in Washington, DC, that are all free to visitors. One of her favorite classes, run by an outdoor education organization, brought students out into the woods every Thursday to learn about edible plants. The more Kallan learned about the environment, the more worried she felt about the world.

Kallan's family helped establish the Climate Stewards of Greater Annapolis, an organization to promote education and advocacy on climate change. Kallan and Reece attended these meetings, and sometimes scientists from local universities or the Smithsonian came to speak.

In 2017, when Kallan would be 13, the People's Climate March was going to take place in Washington, DC. She knew this march would be the largest and most diverse climate march in history, and she had an idea. She was determined to represent the anxiety her generation feels about the future. She landed on the idea to show up as a monarch butterfly. She felt ready to become a girl with wings.

It takes monarch butterflies five generations to migrate 3,000 miles from Mexico to Canada. "They return to the same place each year, but none of the butterflies that migrate there have ever been there," Kallan says. "They fly south along paths taken north by their great-great-great-grandparents." They're not like birds who return to the same place every year. Only the fifth generation of monarchs born will reach the final destination. "So, what will the world be like for the fifth generation of children today?"

"She wanted to carry this giant butterfly with a group of kids," her mom, Kimberly, says. "So her first thought was, *We'll sew it*. But I discouraged this because it sounded like a huge project. That's why we got the parachute and laid it out on the driveway."

Together, Kallan and her family drew giant butterfly wings and scaled them onto a grid on the 24-foot parachute. "My mom free-handed the monarch, and my brother and I spent the week coloring the butterfly in with Sharpies," Kallan says.

Before the march, Kallan got 1,600 kids to sign the parachute. "We took the parachute everywhere and contacted everyone we knew who might be able to help get signatures," Kallan says. "Several schools invited us into their classrooms so students could sign. We collected signatures at the March for Science and also spread it out on the National Mall a couple times and invited passersby to sign." Some kids also wrote down their worries about the future in orange, blue, and green markers.

Then, on April 29, 2017, Kallan "flew" down Pennsylvania Avenue and around the White House. Her butterfly took wing.

It caught the attention of a group called Mother Earth Project, and together they collaborated to create the Parachutes for the Planet initiative. They encourage people across the globe to create their own parachutes to raise awareness about the climate crisis. Kallan's goal was to reach 3,000 parachutes, and as of 2020, she'd helped create more than 3,400 all over the world.

In the summer of 2018, Kallan heard about a girl around her age in Sweden who was striking about the climate crisis every Friday outside the Riksdag, the Swedish parliament. Her name was Greta Thunberg. Four months later, in December, Kallan decided to follow Greta's lead: she registered as the first official Fridays for Future striker in the United States.

In the meantime, Kallan was already working on another big idea. Her state's legislators were considering a Healthy Green Amendment to the

Maryland state constitution to ensure that everyone has a right to a healthy environment. An amendment is a change or addition to a legislative motion, bill, or constitution. As the girl in the wings, she wanted to support the amendment. But how?

Kallan says that her Quaker practice has shown her that silence often speaks louder than words. Quakers begin their meetings in silence as a way to quiet their minds. That's why she decided to hold a silent strike for 90 days. She did not speak, she explains, because adults were not listening. "Because I'm Quaker, I drew some inspiration for this idea from our own silent worship," Kallan says. "I'm used to sitting in silence and waiting for the light to guide."

During an interview with a Baltimore TV station, 15-year-old Kallan replied to questions by writing on a whiteboard. When asked what she wanted lawmakers to do, she wrote, PASS THE HEALTHY GREEN AMENDMENT, which would have made access to clean water and air a constitutional right for everyone in Maryland.

Every day for 90 days, from January through March, Kallan sat silently in the cold on the front steps of the State House in Annapolis and crocheted small butterflies to give away to anyone who passed by.

"The Healthy Green Amendment has yet to pass," Kallan says. "We hoped to get the bill passed during the 2020 session, but the legislature adjourned early due to the COVID-19 pandemic. Unfortunately, a lot of important legislation was not addressed before the session ended."

"Kallan is in this for the long run," her mom says. "Even through ups and downs, she's so dedicated. She doesn't see anything else to work on."

At home, Kallan loves music. "She loves playing the cello," Kimberly says. "Music is very relaxing for her. Every day, she makes time to practice and play."

In September 2019, the United Nations invited Greta Thunberg to accept the Champions of the Earth award. But she couldn't make it to the event in New York City because she was on her way to environmental protests in

Canada. So Fridays for Future asked Kallan and a number of other youth activists from the organization to take Greta's place on stage.

That night, Kallan and her friends stood in front of a huge audience dressed in fancy clothes. They definitely looked like they were out of their comfort zones, but they shyly posed for photos. Then someone handed Kallan a shiny trophy. Kallan shocked the audience when she turned down the prestigious trophy. "Awards are for celebrating achievement, but the achievement we seek has not occurred," she said. "The world is in a climate crisis, and the actions of the United Nations are failing to stop it."

Kallan pleaded with the audience to listen to the science. "There is no denying the evidence. We are experiencing catastrophic storms, floods, fires, and droughts." She raised her voice into the microphone and added, "People. Are. Dying."

Kallan explained why she and the other activists would not take the trophy: "We cannot accept it—instead, we hold it for you to earn. You at the United Nations hold the power to save humanity from itself."

Shreya Ramachandran

Born: August 13, 2003
Lives: Fremont, California, United States
Loves: Solving problems
Instagram: @shreyaramachandran
Pronouns: she/her/hers

In early 2020, Shreya's parents got a voice mail from a producer at NBC's *Dateline*, saying the producer had read an article about Shreya who, when she was 14 years old, had set out to find ways to conserve water. Shreya had just won Sweden's prestigious Children's Climate Prize, so the *Dateline* crew wanted to travel to her home to interview her for a film about the environment.

But her parents were skeptical—particularly her dad, who feared a hoax or a trick.

In the end, the call was very real: a camera crew flew across the country to Fremont, the suburb in Northern California where Shreya lives with her parents. "They were filming the minute before they stepped into the house," says Shreya's mom, Hiran.

The TV newscaster wanted all the details about Shreya's awards, which fill up an entire wall in her home. The Children's Climate Prize, for example, is one of the world's most prestigious climate awards for young people aged

12 to 17. It also awarded $10,000 in US currency for Shreya to continue her work.

The prize committee explained why they chose Shreya: "She is working to save the source of life. What more can we ask from a young talented entrepreneur? Her work is of great significance today but will be even more important tomorrow as water scarcity continues to be one of the world's most important issues to tackle."

Shreya's awareness was raised when she was 12 years old, on a trip to India to visit her grandparents. The land there reminded Shreya of certain parts of California, especially where she'd traveled with her archery team to compete in bone-dry fields, where everything was arid and thirsty after so many rainless seasons.

Shreya knew firsthand about the droughts in California, which in some years of little rain made water expensive and even forced towns to limit water per household. She'd talked to people about how hard it was to find water for drinking, bathing, and watering their crops when there was no rain. "That got me thinking about water and why it's important."

While in India, Shreya noticed a water shortage similar to the one near her home. "Farmers had to abandon their villages and move to cities to find work," she says. "It wasn't just something I read about. This had affected my family, and I saw how much this was hurting my family."

"My mom also told me stories about having to stand in line after school to get water for two hours every day," Shreya says. "I can't even imagine that. It's such a day-to-day struggle! If you see all of this happening in the world, how can you *not* do something about it?"

Back in California, Shreya wanted to know more. "I started to study rainwater conservation methods. But they aren't effective during times of drought, because you can't harvest rainwater if you don't have any rain. That's when I started looking at grey water." Grey water? Shreya describes it as "lightly used water from sinks, showers, baths, and laundries."

There are three types of water, Shreya says:

o   White water: clean water

- o Grey water: used water from sinks, showers, baths
- o Black water: water from toilets

In other words, grey water is water that you've used once in your home and can use again for purposes such as flushing your toilet. (Not for drinking!) "You can use grey water to water, or irrigate, your plants," Shreya says.

Right now, most homes and businesses mix grey water with black water. "So it's all unusable," Shreya says. "I really wanted to focus on how we might reuse grey water on site and save huge amounts of water. That's when I started to look at laundry-to-lawns systems," meaning grey water that could be used to water lawns and plants. "But I realized that many of the soaps have harmful chemicals in them, which harms soil and plants and life," Shreya explains.

What happened next changed Shreya's life: her grandma came to visit her in California. "She brought these soap nuts to our house to make shampoo, and I was fascinated," Shreya says.

Today, many manufactured soaps are made with chemical additives, moisturizers, dyes, scents, and more. Before manufactured soap came to India, people used "soap nuts," actually the dried husks from the soapberry nut, which comes from trees that are native to India and Nepal.

But was the grey water from soap nuts safe for reuse?

"After extensive background research, I couldn't believe no one had researched soap nuts or their grey water!" Shreya says. She set out to find more answers. First, she had to figure out if these soap nuts harmed soil or plants. For the next four years, Shreya found out everything she could about soap nuts and grey water, including researching and experimenting on her own.

For one experiment, Shreya grew more than 100 different plants to test grey water on them. "I wanted the proper lighting and temperature for my plants. The place in our house that was perfect was the master bedroom," she says. "Yes, I kicked my parents out of the master bedroom and turned it into my greenhouse to set up all my plants!"

In a multistep process, Shreya took notes every day to measure the plants' growth and compile facts about them, including the effects that grey water had on soil and plant nutrients and the soil microbiome. She also ensured that grey water irrigation would not contaminate the soil with *E. coli*, bacteria in poop that can cause diarrhea or worse.

"I realized that I needed to analyze my data, so I took a high school statistics class that was really awesome." Shreya was in seventh grade when she took that class!

"Some people asked me why I didn't wait until high school to start my research, or they offered to take the project over for me," she says. Although some people doubted her because of her age, Shreya was undeterred.

"I also read every research article I could find." She emailed professors to ask questions; one professor from the University of California, Berkeley offered to help Shreya make sense of her results.

Shreya found a lab in Santa Clara, a 45-minute drive from her home, where she could grow her plants. "I can't drive yet, so my mom would drive me there every day after school. I'd water the plants, and she'd hang out. On weekends, we'd get there early, and I'd work on my research all day."

"My parents are so supportive, especially my mom," Shreya says. "And bacteria freaks her out! We did a lot of hand-washing when I got home from the lab."

Shreya decided it was time to promote the reuse of grey water to other people. So she founded a nonprofit called the Grey Water Project to promote the reuse of grey water. She also leads seminars to show people how to build grey water systems. She has even written a grey water lesson plan for elementary students so they can learn about water conservation.

In the meantime, Shreya is also the youngest member of Fremont's Environmental Sustainability Commission. "I bring the youth voice to the city. Those meetings can go late!" Shreya laughs. She's currently helping the city put together a new climate plan.

Shreya's work wowed the jury of the Children's Climate Prize. "Almost half the water used annually in a typical household—about 73,000 gallons—can be reused to water lawns and gardens," the jury said. "Shreya built her own grey water cleaning system with soap nuts—which makes grey water reusable. She now teaches others how to install their own systems and holds regular how-to workshops on water conservation and reuse."

Shreya has won many science awards for her work, including being one of the top 20 global finalists for the Google Science Fair and third place at Intel ISEF, the International Science and Engineering Fair.

In 2020 the California Life Sciences Institute moved its awards ceremony online due to the COVID-19 pandemic. It announced that Shreya was the winner of the Bay Area BioGENEius Challenge, a competition that rewards outstanding research and innovation in the biotechnology field. "Shreya was so stunned. She was staring at the screen," her mom says. "She doesn't expect any awards, and I was screaming more than her!"

There's another honor that makes Shreya happy, and it actually goes back to middle school, when she was in eighth grade. The Lincoln Laboratory at MIT (Massachusetts Institute of Technology) had discovered a host of "minor planets," also called asteroids, but they had no names. MIT decided to name the asteroids after the United States' first- and second-place finalists who'd competed in a Broadcom MASTERS, a math and science competition. So, somewhere out in space today, there's a minor planet on quite a trajectory. It goes by the name of "33188 Shreya."

Jamie Margolin

Born: December 10, 2001
Lives: Seattle, Washington,
United States
Loves: Rewatching *Birds of Prey* and
the animated series *Harley Quinn*
Instagram: @jamie_s_margolin
Pronouns: she/her/hers

Mitch Pittman

During recess in second grade, Jamie Margolin handed out SAVE THE EARTH pins to kids and told them, "Join me if you care about saving the Earth."

Jamie wasn't exactly sure what would happen in her Earth Club, but she knew that she had to *do* something. "I was that nerdy kid who grew up watching nature and science shows," Jamie says. But as she got older and read more, she knew she had to act—because people in power were not just killing the Earth; they were killing every living being on it.

By the time Jamie started high school, she'd joined Plant for the Planet, an organization in Seattle that gives a platform for youth to speak out about the climate crisis. In 2017 wildfires in Canada blew smoke over the Pacific Northwest, and Jamie felt sick from all of the thick gray smog. Many of her friends complained about sore throats and headaches.

That's when Jamie started testifying, or giving evidence, at hearings in her state government. With the help of the organization Our Children's Trust, Jamie and 12 other young people sued the State of Washington for denying youth their "constitutional rights to life, liberty and the pursuit of happiness by actively worsening the climate crisis." Jamie says her generation has a constitutional right to a livable environment.

"By the time summer vacation after my freshman year rolled around, I was a fully fledged activist who saw through everything that politicians and industries had told me all my life," Jamie says. "I wasn't afraid to speak truth to power."

Still, Jamie's worries didn't go away. Some nights she couldn't sleep. She worried about the future ahead and what her life would look like growing up in a world shaped by the climate crisis. She worried about every beautiful place she'd ever been to. She worried about every beautiful living creature she'd ever seen. How would we survive if we went on like this?

Jamie grew very sad. "I was so petrified by this massive crisis that I completely shut down," she says. "The impending destruction of life as we know it was too much for me to bear."

In 2016, Donald Trump became president of the United States and said he would withdraw from the Paris Agreement, a declaration to prevent a global temperature rise of 2 degrees Celsius (3.6 degrees Fahrenheit). "This changed everything for me," Jamie says. "After Trump won, I'd had enough."

Jamie signed up for a three-day training with former vice president Al Gore to become a leader with his Climate Reality Project. This meant that Jamie joined a big group of people, mostly adults, to learn about the science behind the climate crisis and how to find solutions. "I decided to take my local activism to the national level," Jamie says. "I had a vision of young people marching in the streets, demanding climate justice. I was going to make it happen."

Jamie was 15 years old when she founded a national youth movement called Zero Hour because "we have no more time to wait around." She organized a group of youth activists from all over the world and found sponsors, such as the Sierra Club and 350.org. Her nonprofit organization's goal was to educate people about the climate crisis and get more people involved to create change. Jamie knew that if young people—even if they weren't old enough to vote—came together all over the country, their voices would be loud and clear. Zero Hour has organized marches in more than 25 cities and met with lawmakers because everyone deserves a livable future.

In 2018, one month after Zero Hour got off the ground, Greta Thunberg began her own solo climate strike in Sweden. Many of the youth who organized the Zero Hour marches are now Fridays for Future organizers and strikers with Greta.

Jamie says that her brave, strong-willed mom, Janeth, who emigrated from Colombia, along with her Jewish American dad, Mark, instilled in her a pursuit for justice. "My mom is the strongest person I know," Jamie says. "She has been through such a hard upbringing of poverty and trauma."

Jamie's mom gushes with pride about her daughter. "She's so creative!" Janeth says. "She's always surprising me. 'Look, Mom, I wrote this article in this newspaper, and this one in this magazine.' And now she's written a book!" Jamie always dreamed about writing a book, and in summer 2020 her dream came true. *Youth to Power: Your Voice and How to Use It* was published in June 2020. Greta Thunberg wrote the foreword.

Yet, like any mother-daughter relationship, Jamie and Janeth's is not always easy. "My whole Colombian family wishes I wasn't so publicly open about being queer," Jamie says. "We get into fights about that. My mom is worried that I'm exposing myself to discrimination. I argue that I am trying to be an LGBT Latina role model for others, one I wish I'd had." Jamie dedicated her book "To the queer kids. We are unstoppable."

Jamie refuses to let others try to fit her into one box. She describes herself as a Latinx, Jewish, queer woman. She refuses to stay silent. She refuses to sit down when people around her are oppressed and marginalized. Jamie has written opinion pieces for the *New York Times*, *Time* magazine, CNN, and the *Guardian*. *Teen Vogue* listed Jamie as one of 21 under 21 young women who are changing the world. In 2019, Jamie was also the winner of an MTV EMA Generation Change Award for her activism.

Before COVID-19, Jamie got up at 5:30 AM every weekday to work on Zero Hour, emailing and posting on social media. She got to school by 7:00

AM, an hour early, "to finish the homework I didn't get to the night before and cram for all the tests and quizzes I hadn't studied for because I was on conference calls."

Every day, her phone buzzes with alerts, questions, and problems to solve, like *"Hey Jamie, check your email I think there may be a big problem . . . we might have upset the leader of the House Natural Resources Committee."*

"I try to focus in class, but my head is usually spinning," Jamie says. "How am I supposed to plan and care about my future when my leaders aren't doing the same?"

After school, it's back to organizing. "This is when we have our big important calls to plan and strategize," Jamie says. "I take the Seattle public bus system back home, so all of this is going on through my headphones on the bus as I ride through downtown Seattle. You could say my natural habitat is the bus system. During that time, if I'm not on conference calls or one-on-one calls, I'm listening to music."

When people ask how she stays grounded, Jamie says, "I have three words for them: Lana. Del. Rey." Her favorite musician, she says, "is a poet."

There's also her mom, who slices up mangos, Jamie's favorite fruit, for her to snack on back home. "I think the greatest sign of love my mom shows me is when I'm on a conference call that's running late, she brings me some cut-up fruit," Jamie says. "If that's not love, I don't know what is."

In 2019, Zero Hour organized a huge Youth Climate Summit in Miami, Florida, where hundreds of youth traveled from across the country to learn how to become climate justice advocates. Jamie and her team raised enough money to make the summit free for anyone under 25 years old. "The team chose to host the summit in Miami because of the huge disasters Miami is already facing and will continue to face with worsening climate change," according to Zero Hour organizers. "With two degrees Celsius of warming, the entire city will be underwater."

Two months into her senior year, Jamie had already traveled all over the United States, as well as to Europe, Mexico, and Spain. She'd spoken to corporations and carved out time for daily media interviews, including with

MTV, *The Today Show*, the BBC, and NBC. But during all of her trips, Jamie was most excited to meet one person: Representative Alexandria Ocasio-Cortez, also known as AOC and the cosponsor of the Green New Deal. There are so many similarities between Jamie and AOC: they're both smart, organized problem-solvers who work hard, cope with crises, and take care of business. Jamie joked that her goal was to go to college on the East Coast so she can be the Jewish Alexandria Ocasio-Cortez. In Washington, DC, Jamie got to meet AOC and give her a big hug.

Also in Washington, DC, Jamie met Greta for the first time; they both testified before the US House of Representatives on the global climate crisis. This meant that Jamie and Greta reported facts to the leaders about how they'd devastated the planet and what they could do to repair it *now*. "I am missing a lot of school to be here," Jamie told Congress. "It's my senior year of high school, college applications deadlines are looming, and to be honest, I've barely started because I'm too busy fighting to make sure I'm actually going to have the future I am applying to study for.

"When your children ask you: did you do absolutely everything in your power to stop the climate crisis, when the storms were getting worse and we're seeing all the effects," Jamie asked, "can you really look them in the eye and say, 'No, sorry'?"

Imogen Sumbar

Born: June 17, 2003
Lives: Bomaderry, Australia
Loves: Snorkeling, hiking, and playing the guitar
Instagram: @imogensumbar
Pronouns: she/her/hers

Eastern Australia was on fire. It was November 2019, summer in the Southern Hemisphere. It was also one of the hottest, driest summers that 16-year-old Imogen Sumbar had ever experienced. Three miles from her home, thousands of firefighters battled the blazes.

Fire officials described the "tinderbox-like conditions," meaning everything was ready to ignite at the slightest spark. Smoke filled the sky. The winds were so strong they brought down a helicopter that was dropping water.

"Honestly, I have never felt fear like that before," Imogen says.

For days, she stayed inside with her parents. Everyone tuned in to the news. "All we could do was refresh the Fires Near Me app to see how close they were getting, to listen to the radio, and just hope that everything was going to be OK."

As the fires got closer, Imogen stayed on the phone with her best friend in town, as families debated if and when they should evacuate. "They predicted that it was going to move south and push fire toward us," Imogen says. "My friend and I both looked outside, and the sky had turned a dark orange. It looked like we'd entered a dystopian world."

Imogen lives in the small town of Bomaderry, a name that comes from the Aboriginal word that means "fighting ground" or "running water." Wildfires there are not new, but every summer, as the Earth's temperatures rise, it's been getting hotter in Australia. The droughts are longer, making the bush drier and ready to catch on fire.

The Australian government has released reports showing how the droughts and drier weather are connected to wildfires. Climate scientists in Australia have been speaking for years about the links between global warming and spiking temperatures. Even so, Imogen has watched people going on with their lives. "The government and citizens of Australia were warned this was going to happen, but still no one would listen," Imogen says. "I am not trying to blame anyone for these fires, but it was just so frustrating."

In fact, just eight months before these fires blazed near Imogen's home, she'd participated in her first climate strike at a park nearby. People of all ages came together with signs that said GLOBAL WARMING IS A METHOD OF MASS DESTRUCTION. As they chanted together about rising temperatures, it was as if they saw the future.

"We've been trying to educate people, to tell them that natural disasters like this will happen if we don't try to reverse the crisis, but it feels as though no one wanted to listen," Imogen says. "So, when the fires hit, it honestly wasn't a big surprise to me. I knew this was going to happen."

This is also what fueled Imogen to get involved in the Stop Adani movement, to prevent the Adani Group, an Indian energy company, from building the biggest coal mine in Australia's history. The mining and burning of coal is one of the leading causes of climate change. According to StopAdani.com, if built this coal mine would:

o *Destroy the ancestral lands, waters and cultures of Indigenous people without their consent.*

o *Allow 500 more coal ships to travel through the Great Barrier Reef World Heritage Area every year for 60 years.*

o *Get access to 270 billion litres of Queensland's precious groundwater for 60 years, for free. . . .*

o *Add 4.6 billion tonnes of carbon pollution to our atmosphere.*

After the heat waves, droughts, and wildfires of 2019, many Australians have become more aware of the threats of rising global temperatures. "Although I wasn't impacted as harshly as some people by the recent fires, I personally watched my community get hit hard," Imogen says, explaining that the fires got very close to her town, and her community was grateful that they didn't lose any homes. "I saw a loss of biodiversity in my region, and I also experienced real emotions of fear for my family and friends, as well as disappointment in our government." Animal rescuers are still trying to estimate how many millions of animals were killed during the wildfires. The bush areas near Imogen's town are home to kangaroos.

Imogen's dad, John—who drives a tractor for the local city council, mowing fields and maintaining recreational areas—describes this time as "devastating." "It was horrible knowing lots of families that had lost their homes," he says. "I did a lot of work in this time with my employer, controlling areas that were under threat. I spent a lot of time away from family, working long hours. We as a family were OK, though, luckily."

By early 2020, Australia was recovering from the months of wildfires. "Even though there was so much adversity, I also experienced a sense of hope and spirit through locals being there for each other and picking each other up after heartache and devastation," Imogen says. Her dad was teaching her how to drive, so they'd circle around town with heavy hearts, seeing the effects of the fires. "People are starting to get back on their feet," Imogen says. "But people around here are also very conservative and very stuck in their ways."

She and her dad pointed out how the grass and plants were growing back in the land that had burned during the fires. They talked about where to go from here and how to create change.

Imogen has three older siblings who are all adults, so she grew up almost like an only child, her dad says. John describes her as "caring and respectful." "We spend a lot of time together," Imogen says about her dad. "The beach is about 10 minutes away, and we love to snorkel." One of their favorite spots is Jervis Bay, with some of the whitest sand and clearest water in the world.

Yet when Imogen first started organizing demonstrations for the climate, "my family was quite hesitant," she says. Her dad agrees: "Honestly, I wasn't sure how I felt the first time she went to the strike." But John decided to join her on her third strike. "I was very proud of how and why she was doing it." Imogen says she's proud of the fact that her parents' eyes are opening. For the first time, they're talking about how they can take care of the environment and what leaders need to do if Imogen and other young people are going to have a future.

By March 2020, after eight months of wildfires blazing throughout the country, Australian firefighters had extinguished all active bush and grass fires. "In my region, fires burned for 74 days straight," Imogen says. "But this week, we had rain. A lot of rain."

When it rains, Imogen picks up her guitar to play. "I'm also trying to learn piano, but I think I'm a string person!"

Bella Lack

Born: November 27, 2002
Lives: London, England, United Kingdom
Loves: Hiking in nature
Instagram: @bellalack
Pronouns: she/her/hers

At age 17, Bella had raised enough money to produce *Losing Wild*, a short film she wanted to make about how disengaged young people are from the natural world. On her own, Bella had launched the Kickstarter project from her home in London, found a camera crew, and written the script.

"We are in a crisis," Bella says. "A crisis of changing climate, disappearing species, threatened human welfare, and vulnerable civilizations."

But COVID-19 paused her plan. Bella postponed her film to shelter in place with her mom and her older brother and sister. This pandemic symbolizes everything Bella has always thought: "Our fate is bound up with that of other species, and harming them will undoubtedly harm us." She adds, "We need to see ourselves as endangered; that's what we are."

In other words, human lives are deeply connected to the lives of all species in the world. We must care for each other if we are going to survive.

Bella's mom, Susannah, says her daughter has always been a sensitive child who loves animals. "I remember wondering why there was sugar in little piles around the kitchen on the floor and trails of it from just outside the back door into the house. According to Bella, this was to encourage the ants to come in and join us in the house. 'Pets,' as Bella called them."

Bella was 11 when she watched a video about baby orangutans who'd been orphaned after people cut down their habitats to plant oil palm trees. That's when she decided she had to tell everyone about palm oil, which is an ingredient in everything from shampoo and cosmetics to food and cleaning products. Bella created a Twitter account, and for the first year, she had 10 followers. She told those followers everything she learned: how the world's most biodiverse forests have been cut down to grow oil palm trees, destroying the homes of already endangered species, such as orangutans, pygmy elephants, and Sumatran rhinos.

The more Bella read, the more she realized how many animals around the world were suffering. She set up a petition to ban the use of wild animals in circuses in England and Northern Ireland. In 2019 a bill was passed into UK law to protect wild animals such as elephants, lions, tigers, monkeys, and more. By the time Bella was 16, people in England had started to call her "the girl who helped ban wild animals in circuses."

Around this time, French filmmaker Cyril Dion reached out to Bella through Twitter. He asked if she wanted to be part of the movie he was making, a feature-length film called *Animal* about "an extraordinary quest: to find another way to inhabit this planet." At first, Bella thought the message was some kind of joke. But Cyril didn't give up. He told her that English primatologist and anthropologist Jane Goodall had signed on to the film, and then Bella realized this was for real.

Bella took a year off from her all-girls high school in London to travel around the world and film *Animal*. "I've learned a lot more this year about humans and life just being out of school," Bella says. "I've also realized from this year away how much our education system is lacking and how we can change this. This narrow path of education in schools doesn't allow people to connect with nature and learn about the environment."

Cyril describes Bella as "incredibly mature. She also has a great sense of humor. We met some great scientists and political leaders all around the world, and they would take me aside and say, 'Who is she? Is she really 16?'"

Bella and Jane Goodall met for the first time in Paris, where they filmed for two days. "It was one of the most extraordinary conversations I've ever heard between a younger and older person," says Callie Broaddus, a US-based wildlife photographer and founder of Reserva, an international youth-funded land trust. When Bella needed a chaperone to film in Paris—because she was under age 18—Callie stepped in to be there. "Bella was the one who convinced me to leave my stable job at National Geographic and launch Reserva, and gave me that final push I needed," Callie says, explaining how she and Bella first connected in 2019.

Today, Bella is Reserva's youth director. Together, Bella and Callie, with young people from around the world, are raising money to buy thousands of acres of rainforests to protect in the world's first youth-funded nature reserve. Bella is also the youth ambassador for the Born Free Foundation, Save the Asian Elephants, and the Jane Goodall Institute.

During a 2019 TEDx Talk, Bella said, "Nature was never just a hobby or passion for me, it was a necessity. I had such a deep respect, such a deep reverence for nature."

Bella's mom says that Bella writes her speeches on her own and only comes to her mom if she needs an audience to practice. "Yes, she's a writer," filmmaker Cyril Dion agrees about Bella. "She writes so well and so deeply. She understands the complexity of things."

Today Bella has more than 150,000 followers on Twitter. She also writes a blog called Call from the Wild. "If we wage war against nature," she wrote in one entry, "we are waging war against humanity also."

As COVID-19 kept Bella sheltering in place, she said, "In a few short weeks, our species has retreated from the constant gnawing labor of routine and we've become untethered. We are all enduring the uncharted waters of this storm together, but this isn't just about preparing for another pandemic. It is about bettering the core of our humanity, redefining our values, evaluating our situation and envisioning a better future for all life on Earth."

Bella reads the news every day, including everything Jane Goodall says, like: "If we go on treating animals the way that we are, that is going to hit back on us, as it has." This is exactly what Bella has been saying for as long as she can remember: demolishing nature and killing wildlife has led to our own human devastation.

When the world opens up again, Bella plans to make her film *Losing Wild*. In the meantime, she sometimes heads over to Kew Gardens to stroll past the budding hydrangeas, tall perennials, and climbing honeysuckle. But her favorite destination in London is a place called Richmond Park. "I walk there almost every day, for a long time. Right now, there are deer all out in the park. You can hear them roaring. No one else is around."

Malaika Vaz

Born: April 13, 1997
Lives: Goa, India
Loves: Exploring wildlife habitats around the world
Instagram: @malaikavaz
Pronouns: she/her/hers

"I am Malaika Vaz, a wildlife explorer." This is how Malaika, a filmmaker from India in her early 20s, introduces herself at the beginning of each episode of *On the Brink*, a television series about lesser-known and endangered animals in India that runs on Animal Planet and the Discovery Channel.

Malaika tells viewers, "I'm traveling across the country, unraveling the mysteries it holds, hidden wild places, elusive animals, and untold stories. Join me on this adventure as I explore how species survive in the 21st century and meet the people who can't imagine a world without them." Malaika then guides us through a jungle, forest, or desert in search of animals. Thirty seconds into any episode, viewers join Malaika as she treks farther into the wild.

Her program is unique in several ways. An all-women crew made and produced *On the Brink*, a first for Malaika. "We had a woman director, a woman producer, women on the cameras, and women as editors. This wasn't planned. It was such an incredible team to work with!" Malaika says. "Today as a wildlife presenter, when girls watch my shows, I hope they see someone who looks like them and think, *Oh, I can do that, too!*"

As the young woman leading each of the eight episodes, Malaika shows viewers a habitat that people have rarely seen on TV. Most nature shows focus on big mammals, such as elephants or rhinos. Yet Malaika aims to introduce people to the smaller, lesser-known animals in India, like the purple frog, the slender loris, the Himalayan black bear, and the great Indian bustard, which is a type of ground-running bird.

"Malaika is fearless," says wildlife filmmaker and cinematographer Nitye Sood. "Whether she's out in the rainforest pushing her physical limits or investigating illegal wildlife trade stories in dangerous places, she's always got this fearless spirit about her. She has the ability to identify what she needs to do and then not let anything hold her back."

In the episode about red pandas, Malaika hikes in the Himalayas through the snow for most of the day, determined to spot a red panda. "Red pandas are little fur balls, and this has become their biggest liability," Malaika says, explaining that poachers try to hunt them. In the last two decades alone, red panda numbers have halved. In fact, there are fewer than 10,000 left in the wild today. At one point in the episode, Malaika sits in a tree and jokes, "So, red pandas actually come down headfirst, but I doubt I want to try that out today!" Then she picks up some red panda poop and smells it. "This is definitely the sweetest-smelling poop ever!" she says, explaining it's because red pandas eat sweet bamboo.

Malaika grew up in Goa, next to the Indian Ocean. She has always loved spending time outdoors—swimming, hiking, surfing, and horseback riding. She has two younger brothers. Her parents, however, "are not so outdoorsy." Her grandfather used to hunt tigers in the jungles of India. "I was the first one in my family to be interested in wildlife protection," Malaika says.

She was 10 years old when she walked into a local TV channel office in Goa and offered to film an adventure sports show for the TV station. The staff were all amused. But Malaika was serious. She filmed herself horseback riding and brought in the recording to the studio. They loved the show!

For the next two years, she created short films for the station, filming outdoor adventures for Spotlight with Malaika, including segments of her horse riding, windsurfing, and scuba diving. (She's also the youngest certified pilot in India.)

Malaika was 14 when a company called Students on Ice invited her and other youth from all over the world on an expedition to the Arctic and Antarctic. By this time, Malaika was going to a boarding school called United World College in India, where she lived on a biodiversity reserve with students from over 92 countries.

The more Malaika traveled, the more motivated she was to share her experiences. That's why, in high school, along with a few other young people, she founded a nonprofit called Kriyā to expose women and marginalized youth from hostile and vulnerable backgrounds to adventure sports and outdoor education, to help empower themselves and their communities. "We'd all go and climb mountains and just get outdoors," Malaika says about her trips to the mountains, where she watched group members let go of their fears and come home bolder.

Malaika's love for adventure only grew as she got older. "These expeditions became a part of me, and now they're my source of inspiration," she says. "I decided I didn't want to go to college. I decided that what I really wanted was to do was work as a wildlife researcher." Kriyā is still running, through Malaika's school.

Malaika wanted to use film to tell stories because it seemed like the best way to show how people live alongside wildlife and to motivate others to protect the environment.

"She was the young, idealistic, bursting-with-new-ideas-and-energy person at the office," says Nitye, the wildlife filmmaker, who first met Malaika when she was an intern at a wildlife film production company.

When Malaika was 19, she became a National Geographic Explorer, joining her heroes Sylvia Earle and Jane Goodall in a global community that, in the words of the National Geographic Society, funds and supports "groundbreaking scientists, conservationists, educators, and storytellers." Malaika used the money from her first Explorer grant to film a documentary on the community-led conservation of big cats.

Malaika gave her first TEDx Talk at age 20, about her trip to Antarctica. That's where humpback whales captivated her and where she learned they'd been driven to near extinction. "I realized right then that I never wanted to live in a world where we don't have majestic species like whales," Malaika said. "In that moment, I knew I wanted to be a storyteller. I wanted to communicate an experience like this to the world around me."

On one of Malaika's most recent trips to Indo-Burma, she filmed traders transporting manta rays, one of her favorite marine animals. She knew this wasn't legal, so she started to ask questions. She uncovered what she called "a debilitating trade in wildlife products for traditional wildlife medicine" that ended with manta rays being sold in wildlife markets in Guangzhou, China. "I realized that it was up to me to investigate this further." So Malaika traveled alone to the east coast of India. "Globally, the trade in illegal wildlife products is the fourth largest, after drugs, arms, and human trafficking. It's estimated to be valued at billions of US dollars each year."

Malaika went undercover to interview fishermen who illegally caught manta rays to eat. Posing as a seafood trader in Hong Kong, she made business cards and wore undercover glasses to covertly film her conversations. "One fisherman took me to this dingy landing dock, and I saw all of the manta rays he'd caught. I've dived with rays before, so I know how amazing they are," Malaika says with urgency. "It shocked me to see many rays are being killed." Endangered species should be protected, not sold in markets, Malaika adds. "It's time for us to push for the end of the wildlife trade."

Many scientists are showing a connection between wildlife trade and the COVID-19 pandemic as humans invade deeper into the natural world. In fact, in spring 2020, Malaika wrote about "the parallels between climate change and COVID-19" and what "the coronavirus can teach us about the bigger environmental crisis. . . . Here, as with climate change, no single woman or man is an island, and without global action at an unprecedented scale, we all are compelled to completely upend our lives as we know them and suffer severe consequences." She added, "We need to use this moment in time to protect wildlife and ourselves."

In 2020, back on land, Malaika finished filming a new TV series about big cat conservation in India. The show, called *Living with Predators*, was broadcast on the National Geographic channel. She tells the stories of ex-poachers, tribal communities, and forest guards who are conserving the habitats of Asiatic lions, leopards, and tigers. Each episode begins with Malaika driving a jeep into the forest. "I've actually never seen a lion in the wild before!" she says. "So I'm really excited about this."

Sure enough, in one episode, Malaika finds an Asiatic lioness lying down in an orchard. "She's literally five strides away from me right now!" she whispers with excitement. As Malaika interviews everyone in the nearby community who protects these lions, she listens intently as they open up.

"I think one of Malaika's biggest strengths is that she can connect with people," says filmmaker Nitye. "That is what makes her a good storyteller. She can elicit the most genuine responses from people she interviews and get to the crux of environmental issues when she's at work. I think the element of genuineness is what makes Malaika tick."

Malaika has traveled to all seven continents. She has swum around many islands and explored wildlife sanctuaries in every corner of the world. No matter where she goes, her mission is the same: to make us more aware of the precious habitats and wildlife around us so we will want to protect them.

Mabel
Athanasiou

Born: October 21, 2008
Lives: Berkeley, California, United States
Loves: Backpacking in the mountains
Pronouns: she/her/hers

Nine-year-old Mabel unrolled her sleeping bag next to a handful of her fourth-grade friends from Berkeley, California. They were tucked in for the night next to kids from all over Northern California. Some of them oohed and aahed, too excited to sleep.

Were they wide-eyed about the stars in the sky? Not quite. Mabel and her classmates were having a slumber party on the floor of the Monterey Bay Aquarium! Mabel could not take her eyes off the jellyfish lighting up, the sea horses bobbing, or the stingrays swimming in circles. After Mabel and her classmates participated in a project called "Wasteless Wednesdays," the Monterey Bay Aquarium's Ocean Plastic Pollution Summit selected them to take part in an all-day symposium and overnight with students from all over California who'd also been selected for their plastic pollution action projects.

Wasteless Wednesdays was the name that Mabel and her classmates gave to their efforts to reduce the use of plastic in their school's cafeteria. "We collected nearly 300 pieces of metal cutlery through a cutlery drive, and then for six weeks we offered these to students instead of plastic," says Jacqueline Omania, Mabel's teacher at Oxford Elementary School in Berkeley. "We made a huge impact by keeping thousands of disposables from being thrown away."

Every year, nine million tons of plastic make their way from land to sea. It's like dumping a garbage truck full of plastic into the ocean every minute. Marine animals mistake the plastic for food and eat it. Sometimes they get tangled in the trash.

Yet reducing plastic utensils in her school cafeteria was not the only project Mabel did that year to reduce single-use plastics. It all started at the beginning of the school year, when Mabel's teacher played an eight-minute movie, "The Story of Bottled Water," about how Americans buy more than half a billion bottles of water every week. Mabel wanted to know where the bottles went after they were empty. The same went for the plastic in their snacks and lunches. What happened when they threw away all of those plastic bottles and plastic bags?

The class said they wanted to do a "waste audit" of their class trash to see exactly what they threw into the landfill every day. There were plastic mechanical pencils, plastic dry erase pens, plastic markers, and more. Mabel and her friends learned that the plastic they tossed into the class trash never really went away. As a class, they decided not to throw anything away that year.

Mabel came home the first week of school and told her parents they didn't need to buy anything for school. Her teacher spread the word that the class wanted reusable supplies, which is how they connected with a two-woman company in San Francisco called Wisdom Supply Co.

Room 22 created a class website to let parents spend five dollars for the school year on classroom supplies, instead of shopping for individual students, and through Wisdom Supply Co., Ms. Omania purchased items such as unpainted pencils instead of markers. (Did you know that unpainted pencil shavings can be composted?) In place of glue sticks, Mabel and her classmates reused plastic bowls from the cafeteria by filling them with glue and using their fingers for dipping. They also came up with the idea to sew reusable cloth bags to replace the plastic produce bags commonly used in the grocery store.

Mabel and her classmates set out to reduce their trash, and their goal was clear: all of the waste from the entire school year would fit into a one-quart jar. So instead of a trash can in the room, all garbage went into this glass jar.

The students began keeping sustainability notebooks, where they observed, wrote, and made predictions. Being sustainable means not taking more than nature can restore. It also means avoiding leaving traces of your presence wherever you go. So, in her notebook, Mabel recorded data about, say, how much waste her family produced every week at home.

"The kids need to stay positive," Ms. Omania says. "I want them to feel empowered, to know they can make a difference and experience this in public school."

Mabel wanted her class to be the first zero-waste class in the United States. She loved her friends' zero-waste birthday parties with homemade snacks brought to class on baking trays. Their class had no-waste parties for Halloween and Valentine's Day too.

During the school year the total amount of trash accumulated by Mabel's class fit into the one-quart glass jar! That's exactly one quart of landfill waste for the entire 180 days during the whole school year! By comparison, most classrooms in America generate 360 five-gallon bags of waste a year—or even more.

But Mabel and some friends wanted to do more, so they started a chapter of Heirs to Our Oceans, an environmental group dedicated to protecting the world's oceans, led by their teacher. Well, not exactly *led by*. Ms. Omania lets the kids lead.

"Ms. Omania does a great job of giving the kids agency," says Mabel's mom, Joni, a lawyer who's a public defender for youth in the Bay Area. "She allows them to take on leadership roles, and she lets them speak. She doesn't tell the kids what they should say."

For example, Mabel was very excited about the cutlery kits one kid in her Heirs club proposed. "We cut a square out of a shirt we don't wear anymore, and sewed it. It does more than hold your silverware: when you unfold it, it's also a placemat."

Mabel's class was so excited when they began receiving produce from Full Belly Farm, a small organic farm located a couple of hours away, thanks to funding from the Berkeley Public Schools Fund. "This idea allowed students to experience what sustainability looks like: direct connection to a farm and farmer," Ms. Omania says. Twice a month, her students opened up a farm box to learn what was in season. They made menus that incorporated science, math, and new vocabulary. They tasted raw fruits and veggies from the box, and took turns cooking at home and bringing meals to share with the class.

Mabel's parents noticed how their daughter took what she learned into the world. For example, Mabel modeled for her younger sister to say "no straw, please" when they ordered a beverage. She and her sister also said "no thank you" to a plastic lid if they got hot chocolate or an ICEE in a paper cup at the beach. "We just get the paper cup," Mabel says. "No lid, no straw."

Her mom laughs. "I guess that's an environmental ICEE."

Mabel started to speak up at city council meetings, urging leaders to reduce plastic waste. "If 21 nine-year-olds can have a zero-waste classroom, then Berkeley can be a zero-waste city too," Mabel told one crowd.

Even when Mabel isn't at school and taking action with her friends, she carries the zero-waste commitment. Mabel has continued to participate in Heirs to Our Oceans through elementary school, and she now plans to continue with the group into middle school.

One of Mabel's favorite things to do is to go backpacking in the Sierra mountains with her family. "It's so nice! No one else is around!"

No doubt, Mabel will make sure her family's trips to the woods are zero-waste, with a mug full of homemade hot cocoa and a sky full of sparkling stars.

Elizabeth Wathuti

Born: August 1, 1995
Lives: Tetu, Nyeri County, Kenya
Loves: Planting trees
Instagram: @lizwathuti
Pronouns: she/her/hers

In early March 2020, Elizabeth Wathuti left her home in Tetu—a village in the central part of Kenya—to travel to Europe, where she'd been invited to speak about the climate crisis.

At a festival called Elevate, Elizabeth got on the stage in Graz, Austria, and told the audience how deforestation, floods, and the worst locust invasion in 70 years have devastated her country. "The climate crisis in Africa is not a future concern," Elizabeth said. "It's happening right now, and we live it every day."

Elizabeth grew up in the most forested region in Africa, in the highlands of Kenya. "I loved walking to school every morning with trees ahead of me, bushes beside me, the fresh breath, whistling winds around tree trunks, birds singing, and that special feeling of peace and tranquility in nature at its most pristine," she says.

She often walked to the Gura River, the fastest-flowing river in Africa, which is near her home. "I loved sitting at the riverbanks watching the clean streams and rivers flowing through the forests shielded by the natural cover from trees."

Back home, Elizabeth often heard stories about Wangari Muta Maathai, a woman who'd grown up in the same village. Wangari was determined to get an education, even though most girls who grew up in the mid-1900s did not go to school. "While sitting round the fireplace in the evening, my grandmother would share stories about Wangari's work," Elizabeth says. "Little did she know that she was planting a seed in me to emulate this great conservationist."

In the 1960s, Wangari traveled to the United States to study science, then returned to the University of Nairobi, in Kenya's capital city, to get her PhD, or doctor of philosophy, the highest degree awarded by a graduate school. She was the first woman in East and Central Africa to earn a doctorate degree and the first woman in Kenya to head a university department.

"My grandmother valued education so much, and she always encouraged me to study hard just like Wangari, if I ever wanted to meet her," Elizabeth says.

That's why, at age seven, Elizabeth joined the wildlife and environmental club at her school and planted her first tree. "I always loved and admired Wangari's love for the environment, and particularly trees," Elizabeth says. "Our school was located directly opposite a forest, where we would go plant trees during the club days. This made me love nature, and it gave me an opportunity to cocreate with nature and become part of nature."

This was the beginning of Elizabeth's journey to speak up for the environment. In 2004, when Wangari Maathai won the Nobel Peace Prize "for her contribution to sustainable development, democracy, and peace," Elizabeth vowed to study harder. "I had a dream of meeting Wangari, shaking her hand, and planting a tree with her one day," she says. "She used her heart and hands to sow seeds for the future which we are now reaping. She was selfless and fought for the environment with future generations in mind," Elizabeth says.

But in 2011, Wangari was diagnosed with ovarian cancer. She died in September that year.

"Unfortunately, my dream did not come to pass," Elizabeth says. "I was shattered. All my life, I'd worked really hard in school to get to meet her. It was a very sad and emotional day for me. I knew that it marked the end of my dream of ever meeting her."

At first, Elizabeth was so heartbroken that she lost interest in school. "Every effort I'd made to fulfill my dream of meeting Wangari was gone. But something in my inner spirit kept telling me that all was not lost."

Elizabeth went to the library and checked out every book Wangari had written. She discovered Wangari's memoir, *Unbowed*, about her life as a political activist, environmentalist, and single mom of three in Kenya. Elizabeth absorbed every detail, including how Wangari had established the Green Belt Movement to restore indigenous forests across Africa while assisting women by paying them to plant trees in their villages. "This book motivated me and inspired me to stand strong and follow in her footsteps," Elizabeth says. "I may not have met Wangari physically, but her legacy reigns on. I am now, more than ever before, determined to leave my mark just as the late Professor Wangari did."

Elizabeth earned a bachelor's degree in environmental studies and community development, and at age 21 she founded the Green Generation Initiative to help young people become more environmentally conscious by planting trees and learning how to take care of nature for the future.

In 2016, Elizabeth won the Wangari Maathai Scholarship and began to visit schools every week to talk to kids about the climate. "We rise up. We speak up. We refuse to give up without a fight."

Elizabeth's Green Generation Initiative has reached more than 20,000 children in schools across Kenya. She and her volunteers have also planted more than 30,000 tree seedlings through her adopt-a-tree campaign.

It's one thing to plant a tree, but making sure the tree grows is just as important. Elizabeth created environmental clubs in schools so kids could water and take care of the trees every day. "My team and I would always visit the schools every month to check on the progress and conduct more environmental education training sessions." Her planted trees have had a 99 percent survival rate! "Food insecurity has been one of our greatest climate change impacts, and I'm looking to establish more food forests in schools by promoting the planting and adoption of fruit trees."

The year 2019 was a big year for Elizabeth: the Eleven Eleven Twelve Foundation recognized her as the Africa Green Person of the Year. That same year, she won the Green Climate Fund Climate Youth Champion Award, and she was one of the Africa finalists for the UN Young Champions of the Earth. That's not all. The Duke and Duchess of Sussex, Prince Harry and Meghan, also recognized Elizabeth for her work helping kids plant trees to feed their communities.

On a rare quiet weekend when Elizabeth has an afternoon to herself, she walks in the forest and connects with the trees. One person who has witnessed this is Callie Broaddus, a wildlife photographer who left her job at *National Geographic* in Washington, DC, to found Reserva, a land trust to empower youth to make a difference in the future of the planet through conservation, education, and storytelling.

"We planted trees the whole day," Callie says about her visit with Elizabeth. "She really, truly believes in the power of having an early connection to nature, that if children can grow this relationship early on, they'll become caretakers of the Earth and take care of it."

Today, Elizabeth is a youth council member of Reserva. She says the solution to the climate crisis is simple: education. But it's up to leaders to support climate education in schools. "I keep telling the story about the climate crisis in Africa and how it impacts us, hoping that our leaders and the world will act faster before the situation gets worse."

During Elizabeth's trip to Austria, COVID-19 had begun spreading throughout the world. Elizabeth needed to get home to Kenya. She managed to catch one of the last flights to Nairobi, but when she landed, the capital's borders closed. She spent weeks waiting to get back to her family in Tetu.

Elizabeth had never gone so long without seeing her mom. Without a vaccine for COVID-19, schools could not reopen, so visiting students or planting trees was on hold. Elizabeth stayed with friends while working tirelessly online. She considered her time in lockdown as an opportunity to learn and grow.

"The climate and COVID both cause existential threats," Elizabeth says. "They're not isolated, and we can't be silent. At least we can control COVID by social distancing, but if the planet is destroyed, what can we do?"

Elizabeth continues to plead with her government to take action. "Right now, in Kenya, I've noticed that when one issue hits our country, all of the issues that are already there come up. If we ignore one issue, it will still come up. You can't put anything on hold. I will keep up with my weekly climate strikes and campaigns until this becomes a reality. They are not acting fast enough."

Climate One

Sarah Goody

Born: December 27, 2004
Lives: Corte Madera, California, United States
Loves: Listening to musical theater
Instagram: @sarah.goody4
Pronouns: she/her/hers

Fifth grade had started, but Sarah wasn't her usual self. She wasn't sleeping at night. Her mind wouldn't slow down, and by the time Sarah got to school each morning, she was exhausted.

Sarah's parents, James and Christine, wondered where their energetic, upbeat daughter had gone. On top of this, Sarah had been getting awful headaches. They throbbed and wouldn't go away. "When the migraines started, I felt like my life shattered around me," Sarah says.

James and Christine took Sarah to different doctors in Northern California every week to find answers. "I wasn't really going to school," Sarah says. "I spent a lot of time at the hospital, and when that wasn't the case, I either felt sick or just didn't want to be at school."

"We didn't know what was going on," James says.

Finally, one doctor diagnosed Sarah with "stomach migraines," caused partially by eating dairy products.

Sarah stopped eating anything with milk, and her headaches eased. "But everything didn't get better when the migraines ended," Sarah says. "I was still sad."

At school, Sarah says, she hid behind a mask. "I was trying hard to fit in because I didn't want people to think I was depressed. It was so hard and painful going to school every day and putting a smile on my face like everything was all right. No one talks about being depressed when you're in elementary school. I felt so lonely and weird because I didn't understand why I was feeling this way."

By the end of fifth grade, her parents were given an official diagnosis: their 11-year-old daughter had clinical depression.

"It took a long time for me to actually put a name to what I was feeling and call it depression," Sarah says.

Fortunately, Sarah's life changed in sixth grade. That year, her science teacher, Rebecca Newburn, taught her class about the human impact on our ecosystem and how we might find solutions for the climate crisis. For the first time in her life, Sarah realized that everything she loved most—the ocean and woods near her home in Northern California—was at risk due to rising temperatures. Around this time, Sarah and her parents also watched *Cowspiracy*, the environmental documentary about how livestock farming was destroying the planet.

Sarah had already cut dairy out of her meals, but now she clearly saw the relationship between eating animals and the environment. "I felt like animal agriculture had been kept a secret from me. I saw the connection and how it tied to climate change."

Sarah was on a mission: to be an advocate for the Earth. She would speak up. She would raise her voice for the planet. Sarah started to wake up energized. Christine and James were grateful to see their passionate daughter back. Becoming an activist is what saved her life, Sarah says.

The summer between seventh and eighth grade, Sarah signed up for a one-week program in Southern California with youth from all over the world. Youth Empowered Action (YEA) Camp was a place for young people to get resources and tools in order to act on the causes they care about.

Sarah was so anxious as her dad drove to the camp, mostly because she knew no one there. But within 24 hours, Sarah started to meet kids who were like her: sensitive and passionate. They cared about the world too. She'd found her people.

Back home in Corte Madera, Sarah joined Greening Forward, one of the largest youth-led nonprofit organizations in the country. She started to speak up at school. Greening Forward flew Sarah out to a conference in New York City where students learned more about climate activism. That was how Sarah met Alexandria Villaseñor, a climate activist her age who was also born and raised in Northern California. The two bonded over a shared love of musical theater. Also, both Sarah and Alexandria have asthma; the 2018 wildfires in their home state had affected them both, making their symptoms more severe.

Alexandria had moved to New York City with her mom, who was back in school at Columbia University. That's where, in seventh grade, Alexandria started striking in front of the United Nations every Friday by herself with a SCHOOL STRIKE 4 CLIMATE sign. The Friday that Sarah was in New York City, she joined Alexandria's protest, and the two talked about so many things, including the Fridays for Future movement started by Greta Thunberg in Sweden.

Back home again, Sarah realized that no young people were striking in San Francisco. Again, she knew what she had to do. In February 2019, Sarah started to strike every Friday in front of San Francisco's city hall. Later, she moved to the front of San Francisco's Ferry Building. James and Christine supported their daughter leaving school on Fridays, as long as she kept up with her schoolwork. James, a certified public accountant who works in San Francisco, even drove Sarah to the city every Friday on his way to work.

People curiously noticed her, and sometimes they stopped to chat. They wanted to know why she wasn't in school. She had an answer: "Why study for a future that doesn't exist?" Sarah also started to write about her life and the climate. She asked her dad to read her drafts, including an essay she was working on called "Climate Change Activism Improved My Mental Health."

James is very private, so seeing his daughter so vulnerable on the page wasn't easy, even though he felt very proud of her. "I think she's found her own voice," he says, adding that she has outgrown his copyedits.

Teen Vogue published Sarah's essay in April 2020. It read, in part, "Now, I'm a freshman in high school and completely unrecognizable from that sad, lonely girl. I'm hopeful about life again, and I have activism to thank. In fact, I think it saved me."

Sarah also loves to read, everything from dystopian fiction to memoirs. Most recently, she devoured Sara Bareilles's *Sounds Like Me: My Life (So Far) in Song*. "I like her raw honesty," Sarah says. "I find her words very relatable, and the way she writes makes me feel like I'm talking to an older sister."

Between everything, Sarah also founded an organization called Climate NOW, a youth-run group dedicated to bringing awareness to the power of youth in the climate movement. "Our main programs include presenting at Marin County schools about the climate crisis and hosting monthly meetings for students to learn more about environmental initiatives and concepts," Sarah says.

Sarah wants to be there for other young people who might be struggling with depression. Every week on Instagram, she offers her presence and support to anyone who might need to chat. "I'm always here for those who need someone to talk to or just someone to say it's gonna be OK," Sarah says. "Whether or not I know you, we are all human beings, and I will always listen."

When the global pandemic forced everyone to shelter in place, Sarah took her Friday strikes online. Her mom, a nurse, continues to go to work at the hospital, and her dad stays home with Sarah and her brother, who's two years younger.

Sarah continues to write all the time. In spring 2020 she wrote an article for the *San Francisco Chronicle*, pleading with people to face the climate crisis with the same urgency they're facing the coronavirus. "Why aren't we panicking about the climate crisis the way we're panicking about the coronavirus?" Sarah asked. "We all have the power to end the spread of this virus. We also have the power to make change. What I want people to leave with after this pandemic is to see how our actions impact our environment, to start bringing these actions into our everyday lives."

Vanessa Nakate

Born: November 15, 1996
Lives: Kampala, Uganda
Loves: Resolving problems
Instagram: @vanessanakate1
Pronouns: she/her/hers

Vanessa was 22 years old when she stood alone outside the Parliament of Uganda in Kampala to strike for the climate.

After graduating from Uganda's oldest university, Makerere University Business School, with a degree in business administration, Vanessa had started to follow Greta Thunberg in the news, and she felt inspired. So she'd set out to connect with climate activists in Uganda. Unable to find anyone, she began striking by herself in January 2019. "I realized that the climate crisis was one of the biggest threats we are facing right now, even though it wasn't making the headlines in the news here," Vanessa says.

Africa has the least fossil-fuel emissions in the world, but it's one of the most vulnerable continents to global warming.

From there, Vanessa founded a group called the Rise Up Movement to amplify, or strengthen, the voices of activists from Africa. Vanessa explains, "Youth activists of color are often left out of the climate movement."

The world began to notice Vanessa. Later in 2019, she was invited to attend the United Nations Climate Change Conference in Madrid, Spain, also known as COP25. Vanessa wanted to be there to represent her country, where most people depend on agriculture to live. As temperatures rise, droughts and floods increase and destroy the farms people need to survive. "Literally, in my county, a lack of rain means starvation and death for the less privileged," Vanessa told Amy Goodman during an interview with Democracy Now! at COP25.

At one point during the UN conference, Vanessa and hundreds of activists were sent out of the venue because of an inside protest, and the security refused to let them inside to hear the talks. That was the first time that Vanessa experienced what it felt like to be excluded.

One month later, in January 2020, Vanessa received an invitation to attend the World Economic Forum in Switzerland. The forum is an annual international meeting where the world's leaders come together to make big global decisions.

Vanessa, along with 20 youth climate activists from around the world, was on a mission to name the companies, banks, and governments that support and fund fossil fuels. She and her fellow activists camped outside with youth from around the world, and on the last day of the forum, they all marched together. That's when the Associated Press (AP) snapped a photo of Vanessa, along with Greta Thunberg and three other White climate activists from Germany, Sweden, and Switzerland. But when the news agency published the photo for the world to see, they cropped Vanessa out, almost as if she had never been there. The cropped photo showed only Greta and the three other activists, all of them White.

"You didn't just erase a photo. You erased a continent," Vanessa tweeted to the AP. In an emotional video Vanessa recorded, she said, "This is the first time in my life that I understood the definition of the word *racism*."

"This is something that has been going on for a long while, and African activists are trying so hard to be heard," Vanessa added at the Fridays for Future press conference in Stockholm, Sweden. "It gets so frustrating when no one really cares."

The AP executive editor tweeted in response: "Vanessa, on behalf of the AP, I want to say how sorry I am that we cropped that photo and removed you from it. It was a mistake that we realize silenced your voice, and we apologize. We will all work hard to learn from this."

People from around the world reached out to Vanessa in solidarity. "I am stronger than ever," she says.

Being cropped out of this photograph was a clear example of racial injustice in the climate movement and how White leaders have often excluded Black activists and their struggles. Vanessa says she refuses to let this experience define her.

On April 24, 2020, two days after Earth Day and 50 years after the very first Earth Day in 1970, Jane Fonda, a longtime celebrity climate activist, asked if Vanessa would speak to the world about Uganda. Jane Fonda had started a weekly climate protest called Fire Drill Fridays in 2019; every Friday she and some of her famous friends went on strike on Capitol Hill in Washington, DC. The night before her 82nd birthday, Jane was even arrested—her fifth time—while protesting with climate activists.

Since COVID-19 had brought everyone inside to shelter at home, Jane invited Vanessa, who was now 23, for her online Fireside Fire Drill for Earth Day 2020.

"We may not be able to be together in the streets, but it feels so good to be together online," Jane said to the world from her living room. "It means the world to me that you're here, to learn from Vanessa Nakate."

Vanessa told Jane that women are on the forefront of the climate crisis in Uganda. She described the ways that women suffer by, say, having to walk long distances to feed their children, leave their homes, and move due to droughts.

"They don't want to suffer for the rest of their lives. They don't want their children to suffer," Vanessa said. "They don't want the next generation to suffer." She explained that it's the women in Africa who are trying to create change, "because women always stand up for each other."

Vanessa lives with her parents, two sisters, two brothers, and three cousins. She often talks with her uncle, a farmer, about how Uganda has changed over the last two decades because of rising temperatures and how land once used to grow food has slowly turned into desert.

Since graduating from college, Vanessa has sold solar batteries in her father's shop in Kampala, often working more than 60 hours a week. "I'd wake up at around 7:00 AM and go to work until 7:00 PM. I always have a long day, and I get back home when I am very exhausted."

Vanessa works tirelessly to bring renewable energy and eco-friendly stoves to her community. Renewable energy—such as converting sunlight to power—is one simple solution to the climate crisis, she says. If we reduce carbon dioxide emissions, we can protect the world's forests.

One day, someone in Switzerland reached out to Vanessa on Twitter, offering to send money to her to create more solar power in Uganda. "He sent me a message explaining how he wanted to pay to install panels in schools here. At first, I thought it was a joke. But he was real," Vanessa says. The Swiss donor preferred to remain anonymous. He sent the funds, which allowed Vanessa to install solar panels and institutional stoves in a primary school in the Mityana District. This school had no electricity, and teachers used firewood to cook food. "They don't have access to electricity," Vanessa says. That makes it challenging for the school's 300 students to learn.

Vanessa says the solar panels provide enough power for the school's rooms. She adds, "The stoves cut down on the use of firewood to almost nothing. I will also be able to install solar power at the school so students have access to light."

Vanessa has started planning a similar solar and stove installation for another school in Uganda. "Students are also learning about the importance of renewable energy to mitigate the climate crisis," she says. Providing renewable energy to Ugandans is a first step in the climate crisis: "We can't have any more carbon emissions if we're going to have better, healthy lives. We also need to stop deforestation."

In the end, Vanessa says, "greed is one of the leading causes of the climate crisis. The key to solving the crisis is to love people more than profit."

Fortunately, Vanessa is no longer alone. People are listening as she shares the stories and voices of Africa across the world.

Alexsey Reyes

Haile Thomas

Born: December 23, 2000
Lives: Chester, New York, United States
Loves: Dancing and writing affirmations
Instagram: @hailethomas
Pronouns: she/her/hers

Haile Thomas was eight years old when her dad was diagnosed with type 2 diabetes, a disease that affects people whose blood sugar is too high.

Haile's parents didn't want her to worry, but she heard them talking in hushed voices about scary things like heart and kidney disease. So when her mom and dad sat Haile and her sister down to explain why they needed to make some big changes to help their dad get healthy, Haile jumped up. She was ready to help.

Haile already loved to cook. In fact, when she was in kindergarten, her family started to call her "Hurricane Haile" because she pulled out all of the pots and pans, always excited to cook with her mom, Charmaine.

The first thing her family did for Haile's dad, Huey, was cut out all processed foods, such as frozen and fast foods, white rice, and white bread. Before her dad got sick, he'd make himself a bowl of cereal in the morning, but no more sugary cereals for Huey! Now, for breakfast, he and his family sat down to enjoy Greek yogurt parfait with quinoa and chia seeds.

Every meal in their home transformed. For example, instead of cooking the rich meat-filled stews for dinner that they'd had for years, the family got creative by infusing their Jamaican roots into vegetable-based meals like cauliflower chickpea curry.

Eating more fruits and vegetables was a big change, but her dad also started to exercise. In the evening, he and his two daughters watched documentaries about food and health. Within two years, Huey's condition had reversed! He was healthy again, and the family was ecstatic.

Haile says this experience changed her life. At school, she saw that most of her classmates were eating the same foods her dad did before he got sick, like pizza, hot dogs, potato chips, and, yes, sugary cereal. "I realized that the experience I'd had with my dad was important to share with other people, like my peers."

First, Haile and her younger sister, Nia, started their own cooking channel. When Haile was nine years old and her sister was five, they launched their *Kids Can Cook* web series on YouTube. They whipped up dishes while their mom recorded them on video. Clearly Haile was comfortable in front of the camera. She would look right at her audience as she explained how to make pizza, which, she added, "might be considered junk food, but it's not going to be junky because we're going to bake it ourselves and put in good ingredients!"

Learning how to cook—and teaching other kids along the way—set Haile on a mission to teach kids how to eat nutritious food. More than anything, she wanted to show young people how to take care of themselves and take care of the Earth. Haile knew changing the way her dad ate and lived had saved his life.

Haile was 10 years old when she stepped on the stage to deliver her first speech for TEDxKids to tell her dad's story. She made the audience laugh when she said she won't go near the kid's menu at a restaurant anymore.

When Haile was 11, the White House invited her to its first Kids' State Dinner, where Haile wowed then first lady Michelle Obama with her quinoa, black bean, and corn salsa recipe in a national contest called Healthy

Lunchtime Challenge. (By the time she was 15, Haile had met Michelle Obama five more times!) The Hyatt Hotel chain then asked Haile to be its junior chef advisor. Next, Haile was invited to be one of the first young chefs on the Food Network show *Rachael vs. Guy: Kids Cook-Off*.

While hanging with celebrities was fun, Haile wanted to make a real difference in the world, especially for kids of color who live in at-risk communities and might not have access to healthy foods. "Kids in underserved communities often experience lack of accessibility to fruits and veggies because there aren't many healthy restaurants or grocery stores nearby that have a wide selection of affordable fresh produce," Haile says.

Haile was in middle school when she and her mom, Charmaine, founded a nonprofit called HAPPY (Healthy, Active, Positive, Purposeful Youth) to teach children about plant-based nutrition through schools and summer camps. Charmaine reached out to business owners and community members, asking for their support to offer plant-based nutrition and education to underserved and at-risk communities. Their organization has served more than 35,000 kids since 2010.

"My mom is amazing," Haile says. "She's my best friend, and we're very similar in a lot of ways. We're both creative, and we like to get things done!"

It was Haile's idea for her family to go vegan. Thanks to all of the documentaries Haile had watched, she knew that avoiding meat and dairy would not only keep her family healthy but also help heal the environment. "It started off as a challenge to see if we could do it, and then we loved how we felt, and also how we're living in a more ethical and environmental way that's aligned with our morals," Haile says. "We're all vegan today!"

In high school, Haile decided to enroll in the Institute for Integrative Nutrition in New York City. At age 16, she became the youngest certified integrative health coach in the United States.

For now, Haile has decided not to go to college, because she believes that what matters most for young people today is investing in their own communities. "After being asked so many times 'What's next for you, Haile?' and 'Where are you headed?' I finally made this decision to enroll in the school of life," she says.

So instead of taking the SATs, Haile wrote a book, *Living Lively: 80 Plant-Based Recipes to Activate Your Power and Feed Your Potential*, a mix of self-help lessons and recipes. Haile calls it "an empowerment cookbook." Her book also features advice from other activists featured in *Girl Warriors*, including Hannah Testa and Maya Penn.

Haile sometimes struggles with perfectionism, so writing her book wasn't always easy. "I got so overwhelmed at times. I needed to test every recipe as least five times. My mom and sister helped me taste everything. My sister loved the 'Straight Fire Mac and Cheese' with carrot potato sauce. It's a little spicy, and she was tasting this one a lot!" Haile laughs.

Every day, Haile reminded herself that she was writing the book to help people nourish themselves, live their best lives, and make the world a better place. "I got really transparent in this book," Haile says, "because we're all human and we're all figuring it out along way."

Haile makes a point to stay positive. Every morning when she wakes up, she writes what she calls her "GTPT LIST." That means "Grateful to Prioritize Today." For example: *Today I want to feel relaxed, healthy, centered, engaged, free.* Also, the screensaver on her laptop flashes the phrase AMAZING THINGS ARE HAPPENING! "I say this in my head when I'm working or stressed out, or even when I'm going to bed. It keeps me positive."

Not a day goes by when Haile doesn't jump up to dance. "I am the WORST dancer but I LOVE IT SO MUCH," she told her Instagram followers. "If I don't dance or listen to music at some point in the day I don't feel like myself."

With Haile in the world, speaking openly and honestly about her challenges and growth, amazing things will surely continue to happen.

Isabella Fallahi

Born: April 18, 2003
Lives: Indianapolis, Indiana, United States
Loves: Watching Star Wars
Instagram: @isabellafallahi
Pronouns: she/her/hers

When Isabella was a little girl, her asthma got so bad that she'd wake up at night and feel like she was drowning.

Isabella's mom lives near a coal-fired power plant called Harding Street Station in Indianapolis, Indiana, so Isabella's asthma grew worse the nights she stayed at her mom's house. When coal burns, particles are released into the air and cause pollution that's linked to many health problems.

During the climate strike in New York City in 2019, 16-year-old Isabella told this story to an audience of more than 300,000 people. In a clear, strong voice, she described how she had to catch her breath at night, how she wanted to scream for help. "I couldn't scream then, but hear me scream now!" Isabella shouted to the crowd.

She stood on stage that day to describe how she has struggled with asthma most of her life. She told the crowd that people shouldn't have to live like that. People shouldn't have to struggle to breathe or take medication every day because coal in their communities is making them sick.

Eight of Indiana's 10 largest power plants are coal-fired. Developers build coal plants near the poorest communities, where they expect the least pushback. Besides causing asthma, burning coal also poisons the water; it can lead to brain damage, heart problems, and cancer.

Growing up, Isabella went back and forth between her mom's and dad's homes. On weekends, she competed in figure skating, and her dad often drove her to competitions. "As she warmed up, I'd sit there and watch her do these jumps," her dad, Sasha, says. "She'd fall down, and that ice is hard! But she got right back up and did it again! She sticks to whatever she does, and she's fearless!"

Because of her asthma, competing on the ice every week wasn't always easy. "My mom lives less than 14 miles away from the coal-generating facility," Isabella says. "Up until 2016, Harding Street Station was pumping out tons of coal per year. Some people live right next to this facility, so this is not just my story. It's true for a lot of people in my home state."

By the time Isabella started high school, she knew she had to act. When she was 16 years old, she got the chance to stand up to the most powerful establishments in the world. She received an invitation to speak at the UN Climate Change Conference in Madrid (COP 25) in 2019. She hoped this meeting would be a turning point for climate justice. But one of the first things she noticed was that Spanish utility companies were official sponsors of the COP talks, and more than 1,800 delegates came from fossil fuel companies around the world, such as British Petroleum (BP) and Shell.

Isabella and about 300 other attendees decided to protest, demanding to have a voice in the climate decisions that were being made by the fossil fuel executives doing the negotiating. "This is a perfect example of why so little progress has been made on addressing the climate crisis," Isabella wrote in *Teen Vogue*. "Global institutions, big banks, universities, and governments are deeply financially intertwined with the fossil fuel industry."

Isabella joined forces with two other climate activists: Helena Gualinga, an Indigenous environmental and human rights activist from the Kichwa community of Sarayaku in Pastaza, Ecuador, and Ayisha Siddiqa, another activist featured in this book, who was born in Pakistan and lives in Coney Island, New York.

In early 2020, they launched Polluters Out. Working together, the three women spelled out their demands clearly: that the United Nations Framework Convention on Climate Change (UNFCCC) refuse funding from fossil fuel corporations for COP26. (These climate talks were delayed until November 2021 due to COVID-19.) "It is time for us to rise against the fractured systems which have put profits and monetary gain over sustainable economic and social systems," Isabella, Helena, and Ayisha say. "In order to do that, we need to kick polluters out, once and for all." They also named the polluters to the world: ExxonMobil Corp., Saudi Aramco, Gazprom, and Royal Dutch Shell, which have exerted 71 percent of global carbon emissions since 1988.

"You may be wondering how a bunch of kids can take on a multibillion-dollar industry," Isabella wrote in *Teen Vogue*. "It won't be easy, but for the first time in history, we are coming together to form a global coalition of youth climate organizations and independent activists from every continent centered around universal demands."

Today, Polluters Out has more than 150 members from over 40 countries around the world, along with the support of scientists who help them form their policy and demands.

After school and often into the night, Isabella joins conference calls via Slack, Zoom, and Google. Isabella communicates with activists in Cuba on WhatsApp because they can't download other apps due to the US trade embargo. Some organizers need to walk into town to access Wi-Fi. Isabella often jumps on calls at three o'clock in the morning.

Her aunt Tadji, whom Isabella calls *Tía*, says she's "blown away" by Isabella. "She's really giving a voice to those who don't have one," Tadji says.

It's not always easy. "Indiana is the middle of Trump country," Isabella says. Racism and xenophobia, or the fear or hatred of people from different cultures, are common. Isabella's father is from Colombia, and her grandfather is from Iran. People have called Isabella names and threatened to hurt her family. "Before this, I was so proud of my identity, of being Iranian and Latina," Isabella says. "I have such a rich heritage, and for a moment, I almost tried to hide it. But I didn't become an activist to be silent. I needed to tell my truth and turn that truth into power. So I started to talk more openly about my experiences."

Isabella and her dad are very close, and he has supported her through the name-calling and attacks. And they are both big *Star Wars* fans. "My favorite character was Princess Leia," Isabella says. "I loved how she was a leader and not afraid to stand up to evil no matter what. She wasn't the typical princess like Cinderella or Ariel who was a damsel in distress. She was a general, and she led a revolution against the Empire. She in many ways inspired me from a young age to step into that persona of standing up against the most powerful establishment no matter what."

During a radio interview on *Science Friday*, a National Public Radio show, the host, Ira Flatow, asked Isabella if she wants to get "into politics" in the future. "Absolutely," Isabella said. "I want to obviously go through the House of Representatives and the Senate, but my ultimate goal in my life is to aim for the Oval Office in 2044. And I hope the politicians today can start making changes to address climate change, so that I have the ability to achieve that dream."

Ira asked, "Do you promise to come on *Science Friday* when you get there in 2044?"

Isabella said, "Absolutely."

Acknowledgments

If you are raising your voice for change right now, thank you. I'm deeply grateful to you for fighting for the future of this planet. I'm with you in resilience.

A forever thank-you to Kara Rota, Senior Editor at Chicago Review Press, for believing in this book from the start.

A great appreciation to Chicago Review Press and the amazing people who contributed their thoughtful edits, designs, marketing and publicity insights, and more: Devon Freeny, Ellen Hornor, Sadie Teper, Jen DePoorter, and Hailey Peterson.

An enormous thank you to Eric Myers, my agent, for being on my team.

To illustrator Ana Copenicker, I'm in awe of how you captured the essence of *Girl Warriors* on the cover.

To every activist in this book, I'm so grateful to you for trusting me. You responded to so many phone calls, text messages, and pleas to answer just one more question.

Thank you to all of the mothers and fathers, brothers and sisters, friends and colleagues (and an even an aunt!) who also answered my questions so openly.

A shout out to Jonah Gottlieb, one of the first activists I contacted, for sharing the first names that got this book rolling.

I want to thank all of the teachers in the world who are environmental leaders in the classroom, with special acknowledgments to Jacqueline Omania and Park Guthrie.

ACKNOWLEDGMENTS

Thank you to all of the climate writers and podcasters who are asking pressing questions about the climate and finding solutions in the face of crisis, such as: Mary Annaïse Heglar, Amy Westervelt, Georgia Wright, Leah Stokes, Dr. Katharine Wilkinson, Mary Anne Hitt, Anna Jane Joyner, Jacquelyn Gill, Wanjiku "Wawa" Gatheru, Dr. Ayana Elizabeth Johnson, Eric Holthaus, Mary DeMocker, and Alexandria Villaseñor.

Thank you to the generous and thoughtful writers in my circle who read my drafts: Mae Respicio, Alex Giardino, Sharon Eberhardt, Laura Atkins, Susie Meserve, Alexandra Ballard, and Kate Schatz.

All the love to my writing group, which has held me for so many years: Suzanne LaFetra Collier, Veronica Chater, Katherine Briccetti, B. Lynn Goodwin, Annie Kassof, and Sybil Lockhart.

Big hugs to these writers I adore too: Rebecca Woolf, Cheryl Strayed, Amanda Hirsch, Shannon Doleski, and Keely Parrack, as well as everyone from Pitch Wars and #the21ders.

Thank you to the mamas of our East Bay Earth Team: Rachel Anderson, Céline Farchi, and Stéphanie Regni (here's to Fillgood!).

And also to Nneka McGuire for publishing "Meet 4 Teen Eco-Activists Hustling to Save the Planet" at the Washington Post (the Lily).

To Nina LaCour for reminding me how important it is to identify defining moments in one's life.

To Jandy Nelson for hosting #magichour on Twitter during the pandemic to keep me writing.

To Premsiri Lewin for holding me.

To my mom, Maureen Micus Crisick, for encouraging me as a little girl to write those first words down on the page.

To Nova Ren Suma, for leading me to this incredible circle of writers who have been with me for years: Amelinda Bérubé, Tamara Mahmood Hayes, Wendy McKee, Shellie Faught, Catey Miller, Melissa Mazzone, Bree Barton, Jacqueline Lipton, TJ Ohler, and Alison Cherry.

So much love to all of my soul sisters in the world: Arden Fredman, Siobhan van Winkel, Tonya Delaney Cauduro, Leila Cranford, Amanda Dora Riesman, Elise Brewin, Sheila Brewin, and Sabine Herrmann

ACKNOWLEDGMENTS

Thank you to this sweet community for being there: Kellie Lund, Ariel Lustig, Dan Lucido, Payal Sampat, Mattison Ly, Sara Shallcross, Megan Jennings, Jeannie Montag, and Ivan and Christin Weber.

So much gratitude to all the yoga teachers in my life who keep me grounded: Adesina Cash (love Hot Spot Yoga Oakland!), Rachel Goldman-Stewart, Monika Kaufman, Raissa Lerner, Zenovia "Zen" Forbes, and Nels Sundquist.

I'm grateful to Chris Hopkins, my partner in this life, for holding me, bringing me that second cup of coffee, and listening to me when I was filled with doubt and worry.

All the hugs and kisses to Mae and Camille, my creative, brave, adventurous nature-loving daughters, and the warriors at my side.

Resources to Explore

The stories in Girl Warriors *reference many climate organizations and several books that might interest you. This list includes these and other resources you may want to explore.*

ORGANIZATIONS

350.org
https://350.org

All We Can Save
https://www.allwecansave.earth

Bye Bye Plastic Bags
http://www.byebyeplasticbags.org

Call from the Wild
https://www.callfromthewild.com

Climate NOW
https://www.climatenow.solutions

Climate Reality Project
https://www.climaterealityproject.org

Earth Uprising
https://earthuprising.org

Earthjustice
https://earthjustice.org

Extinction Rebellion
https://rebellion.global

Fire Drill Fridays
https://firedrillfridays.com

Fossil Free
https://gofossilfree.org

Fossil Free California
https://fossilfreeca.org

Fridays for Future
https://fridaysforfuture.org

Full Belly Farm
http://fullbellyfarm.com

Grey Water Project
https://www.thegreywaterproject.org

HAPPY (Healthy, Active, Positive, Purposeful Youth)
https://www.thehappyorg.org

Heirs to Our Oceans
https://h2oo.org/

Maya's Ideas 4 the Planet
https://mayasideas.com/pages/mayas-ideas-4-the-planet

Mother Earth Project
https://motherearthproject.org

National Children's Campaign
https://nationalchildrenscampaign.org

Polluters Out
https://pollutersout.org

Project Drawdown
https://drawdown.org

Rad Girls
http://www.radgirlscan.com and https://radamericanhistory.com

Reserva: The Youth Land Trust
https://reservaylt.org

Schools for Climate Action
https://schoolsforclimateaction.weebly.com/

Sunrise Movement
https://www.sunrisemovement.org

Wisdom Supply Co.
https://www.wisdomsupplyco.com

Youth vs. Apocalypse
http://youthvsapocalypse.org

Zero Hour
http://thisiszerohour.org

BOOKS

Lack, Bella. *The Children of the Anthropocene*. Penguin Life, *coming in 2022*.

Maathai, Wangari. *Unbowed: A Memoir*. Alfred A. Knopf, 2006.

Margolin, Jamie. *Youth to Power: Your Voice and How to Use It*. Hachette, 2020.

Penn, Maya. *You Got This! Unleash Your Awesomeness, Find Your Path, and Change Your World*. Gallery Books, 2016.

Testa, Hanna. *Taking on the Plastics Crisis*. Penguin Random House, 2020.

Thomas, Haile. *Living Lively: 80 Plant-Based Recipes to Activate Your Power and Feed Your Potential*. William Morrow, 2020.